HAMLYN · COLOURFAX · SERIES

CARTOONS and animation

DAVID MOSTYN

CONTENTS

Tools and a few rules	2
First you start with a body	4
Let's face it	6
A perfect match	8
Zooming along!	10
How to draw animals	12
Crash! Bang! Wallop!	14
Hand lettering	16
Strip cartoons	18
Animation	20
Hasn't Aunty Vera got a big nose?	26
Colouring in your cartoon	28
Backgrounds	30
Index	32

HAMLYN

TOOLS AND A FEW RULES

The tools of the cartoon trade are very simple, and they are easy to obtain. Here is a list of them: paper; a 2B pencil; putty/kneaded rubber; a dip-pen; black ink; brushes; colour; a black felt-tipped pen; a ruler; adhesive tape; a light box; and scissors. Some of these items are a little more expensive and you do not need to have all of them straight away, but that's the basic list. If you feel like adding to it, or you cannot use comfortably anything mentioned, then change it.

Paper You will need two different types of paper – layout paper and cartridge paper. You can buy layout paper in art supply shops. It comes made up in pads, in many different sizes. Cartridge paper can also be bought in art shops. It comes in sheets and in different grades of quality. If you are going to use it for colouring, try to buy as good a quality as you can afford.

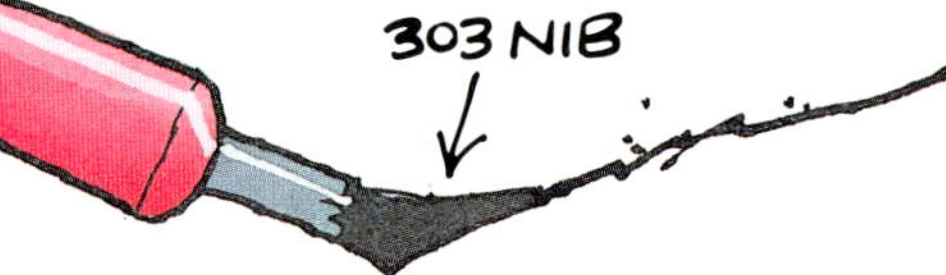

Dip-pen You will need an old-fashioned dip-pen and a few nibs. There are many different kinds of nibs but the 303 is a good one to use, and most shops that sell artists' materials will have them.

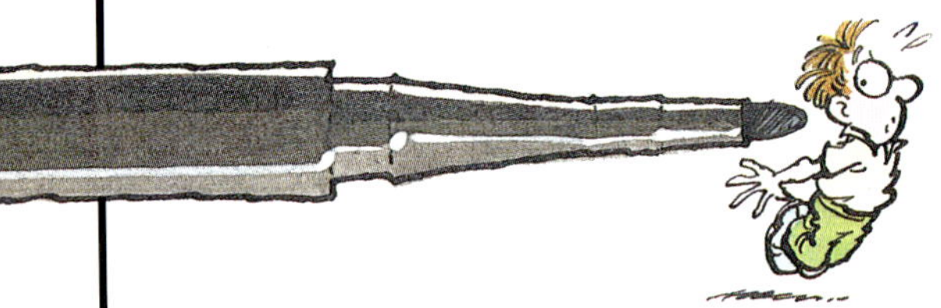

Black felt-tipped pen You can buy these pens in various thicknesses. You should look for a 'fine' point. They must be waterproof. Buy two or three at a time because they do not last for very long.

Pencils Pencils come in different grades. H means hard, B means black. So a 3H pencil would be very hard and 3B pencils would be very soft. A B or a 2B is best. Always sharpen the end of the pencil furthest from the lettering so that, when you pick it up, you know the kind of pencil you have.

Putty/kneaded rubber This is a soft rubber and removes only the pencil from the surface of the paper. A normal rubber will also remove part of the paper, the more you rub. This spoils the paper.

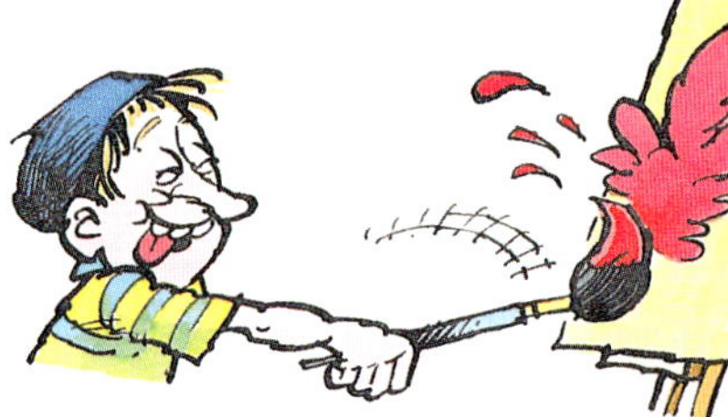

Brushes Brushes should be bought with care. Sable brushes are the very best but they are also the most expensive. Cheap brushes are not worth having. Again, an art supply shop should be able to help if you explain what you want the brush for. You will need two brushes – either number 5 or number 6.

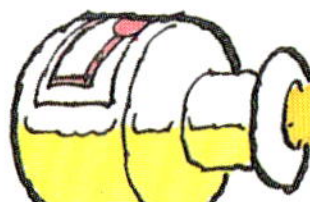

Colour There are many kinds of colouring materials available. Whatever is used should dry quickly. It should not fade in the light, and it should not take a lot of time to mix. Water-based colours, such as water colour or coloured inks, are excellent. Crayons and coloured felt-tipped pens are also very useful. All these materials give very clean, bright colours, essential when producing cartoons.

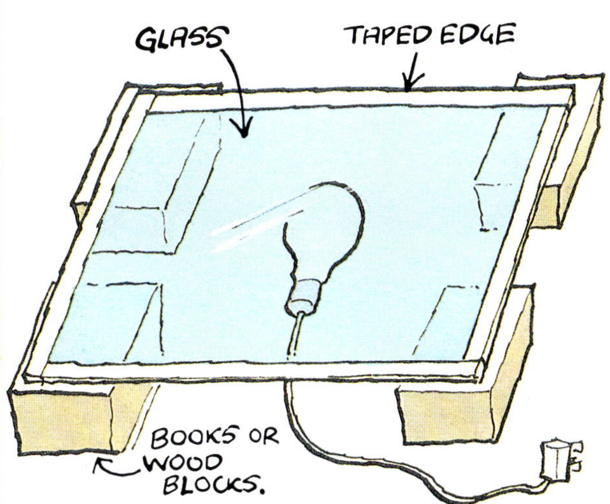

Light box A professional one is expensive, but an adequate substitute can be made quite easily with your parents' help. It is made from a small sheet of glass, a few books, and a light bulb. There is a picture of how it works and you will see how it can be used later. But leave this to an adult. Do not fiddle with glass or with electricity.

A word of warning Remember, you do not need to have all the wonderful (and expensive) equipment that the shops sell. Keep it simple. Abandon anything that you do not feel comfortable with and enjoy the rest.

Ruler Any old ruler will do. Steel ones are expensive but they are better than plastic ones which are easily dented.

Adhesive tape This is good for sticking things to other things!

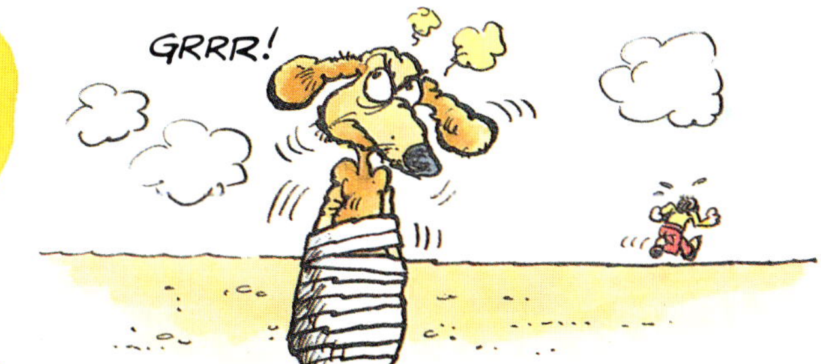

Scissors You may be able to borrow some from your parents.

Black ink You should always buy waterproof ink. One of the brushes will be used for black ink only. But this ink seems to clog everything with which it comes into contact. Always wash out your brush thoroughly when you have finished with it. Even then, not all the ink will come out.

Blotting paper

Tissues

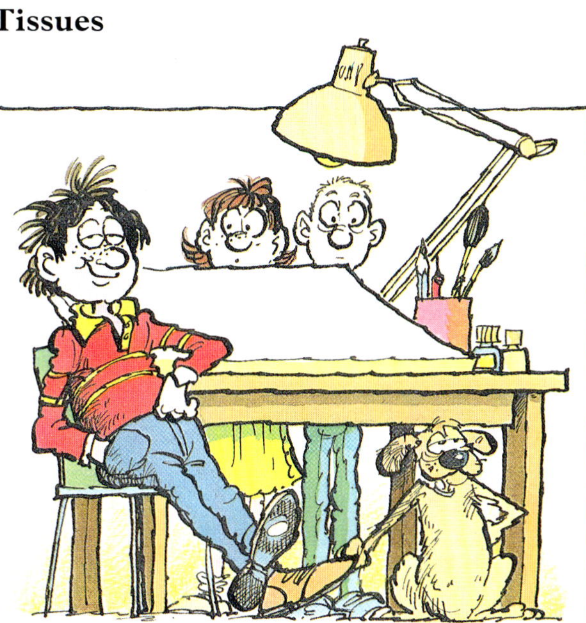

Your studio This is where you work; calling it a studio will impress everyone.

Try to find an old table which is steady. Cover the top with a thick layer of newspaper for protection. A drawing board is useful. If you do not have one, find a piece of wood about 90 cm by 60 cm (3 ft by 2 ft). Put it on the table and raise one side of it on some books. Even some old table legs will do. Cover the board with a sheet of thick, clean card. You will also need a good light over the board.

You have the equipment and the studio; you're ready to start.

FIRST YOU START WITH A BODY

Whatever you do, do not try to draw your cartoon starting at the head and working down. It is a good idea to think of drawing it in the same way as if you were getting dressed. You would not put on your shoes first and then try to get your socks on. You put on your clothes in the correct order until you are fully dressed. It is the same with drawing a cartoon. There is no short cut to doing it. You start with the basic construction and then build on it until you have a complete drawing.

This section describes how you build that first, basic construction. You should make these drawings on thin layout paper.

- Heads are generally egg shaped, so draw an egg.
- Put in a neck.
- Draw a rectangle for the body.

For the arms, draw in two sausage shapes with flat ends, the lower ends reaching to where the top of the legs will be.

Draw in two more sausages with flat ends, and make them a bit longer than the arms. These are the legs.

Draw two mittens, thumbs inwards, on to the ends of the arms. You have drawn the hands.

Similarly, for feet, draw two flat ovals on to the ends of the legs.

Now we can start to make the body look better. At the moment, the shoulders look as though there is a coat hanger in them, so slope them down a little. Make a waist, too, about half way down the rectangle. Look at your own arms. They go in a little at the elbows, and in again at the wrists. The legs, too, should go in a little at the knees and ankles. Make the

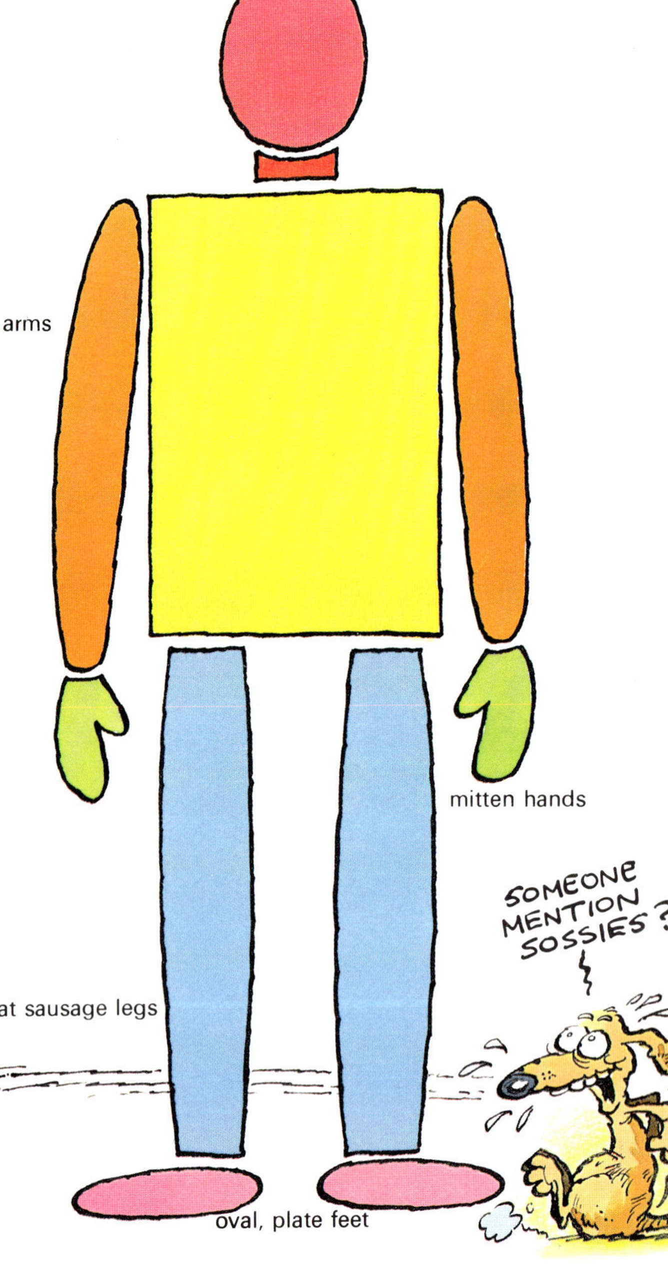

legs meet at the top where they join the rectangle.

Now you are thinking that you have never seen a real person who looks like your drawing. This is where you use your light box. Take this first drawing that you have just made, lay it flat on the glass, and put another sheet of paper on top. With the light switched on you should be able to see your first drawing clearly through the top sheet.

If you want to have another go at it, take another sheet of paper and trace a better figure through on to your new sheet. If you are still not happy, simply try again, and again, as many times as you want.

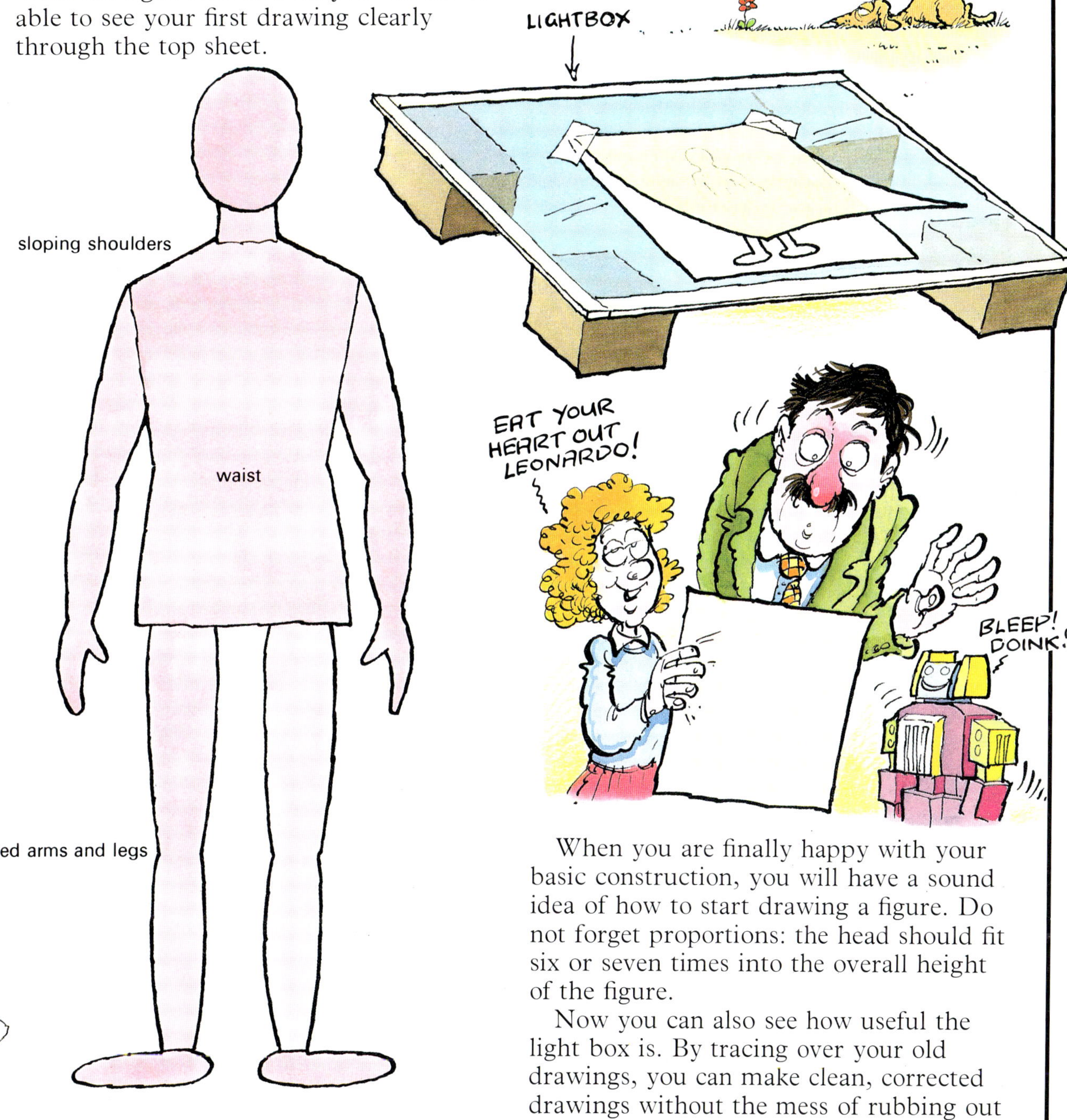

When you are finally happy with your basic construction, you will have a sound idea of how to start drawing a figure. Do not forget proportions: the head should fit six or seven times into the overall height of the figure.

Now you can also see how useful the light box is. By tracing over your old drawings, you can make clean, corrected drawings without the mess of rubbing out all the time.

LET'S FACE IT

Now you have a good idea of how to build up the framework of the body, it's time to go further. Let's start with the face.

All you need is a series of circles, one circle for the nose and two for the eyes. Put in a line for the mouth. Now you have to decide what kind of person you want this figure to be.

Why not decide to draw a big, fat, happy man? So, draw a big smile where you had a straight line before. He really looks happy.

Here's an example of a smiling face going through a series of mood changes: sad; angry; surprised; laughing.

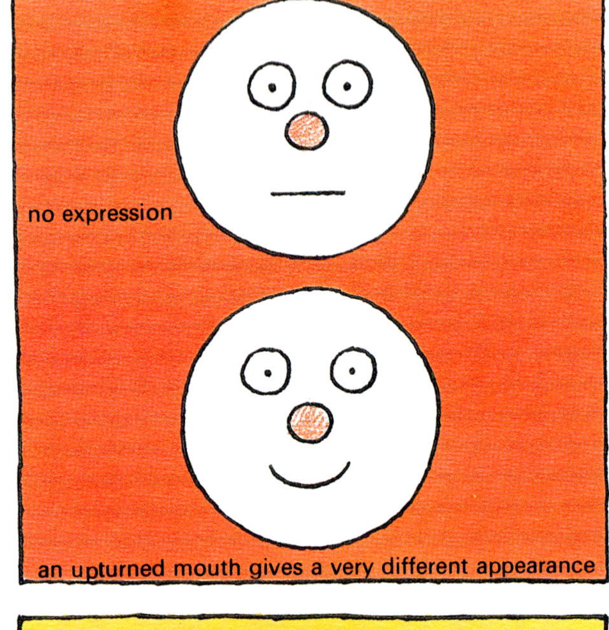
no expression

an upturned mouth gives a very different appearance

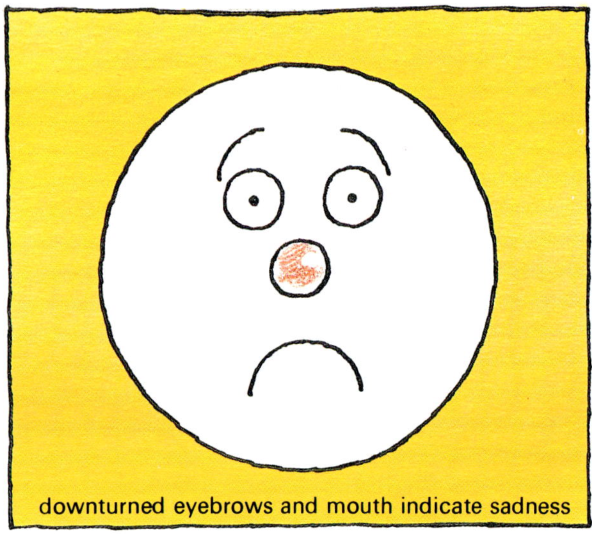
downturned eyebrows and mouth indicate sadness

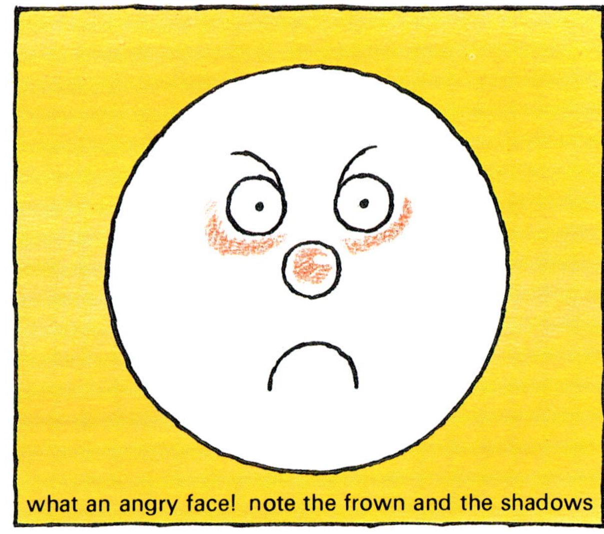
what an angry face! note the frown and the shadows

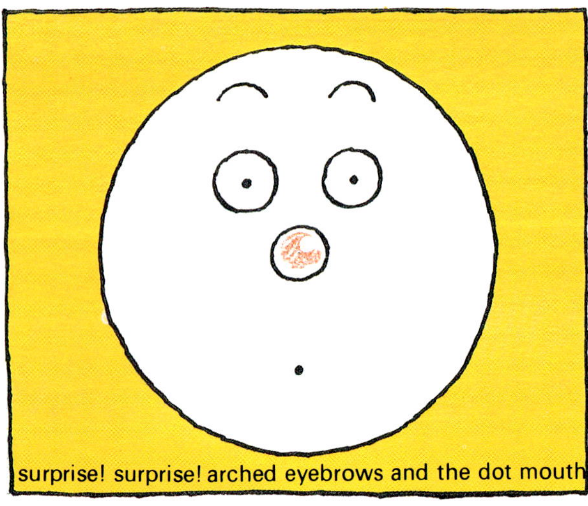
surprise! surprise! arched eyebrows and the dot mouth

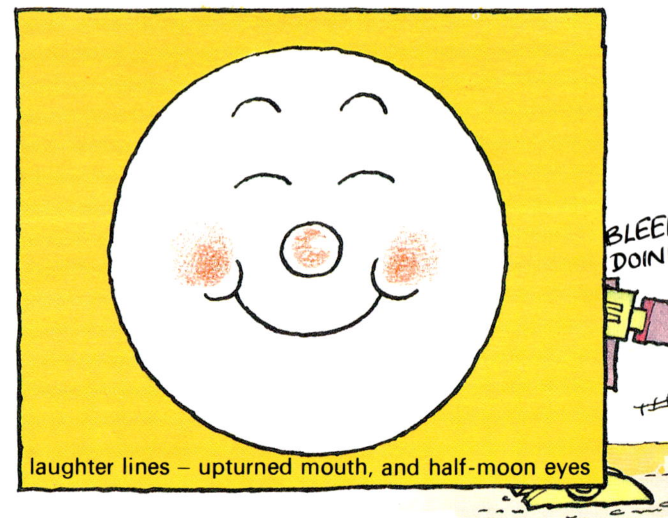

laughter lines – upturned mouth, and half-moon eyes

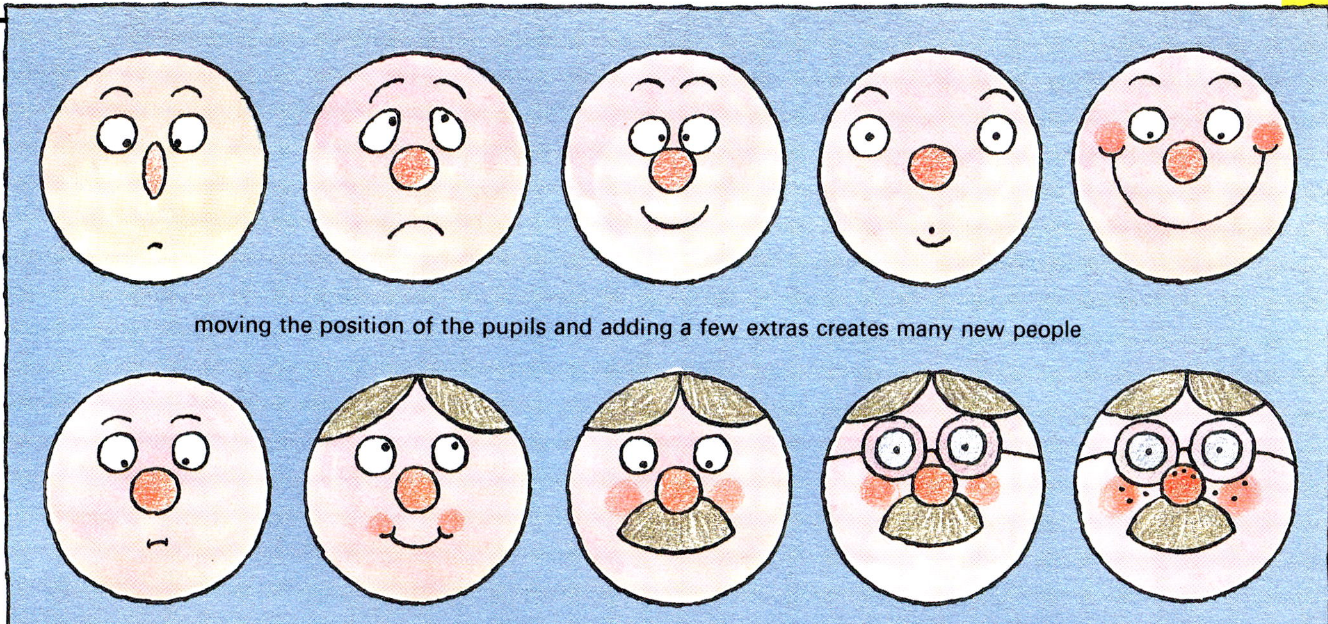
moving the position of the pupils and adding a few extras creates many new people

Once you have drawn your basic construction, you can do whatever you like with it. Change the shape of the nose. Then change the eyes. Try moving the eyes closer together and then further apart. Try the mouth. Make it very wide. Now make it very small. Try different hairstyles. Put moustaches on some of your men. Add a pair of spectacles. What about some freckles? And, don't forget to move the eyeballs around.

Now try changing the shape of the head. You can still begin with a circle but, once you have done that, make it wider at the top and narrower at the bottom. Then try it the other way round. You can spend hours inventing different-looking people.

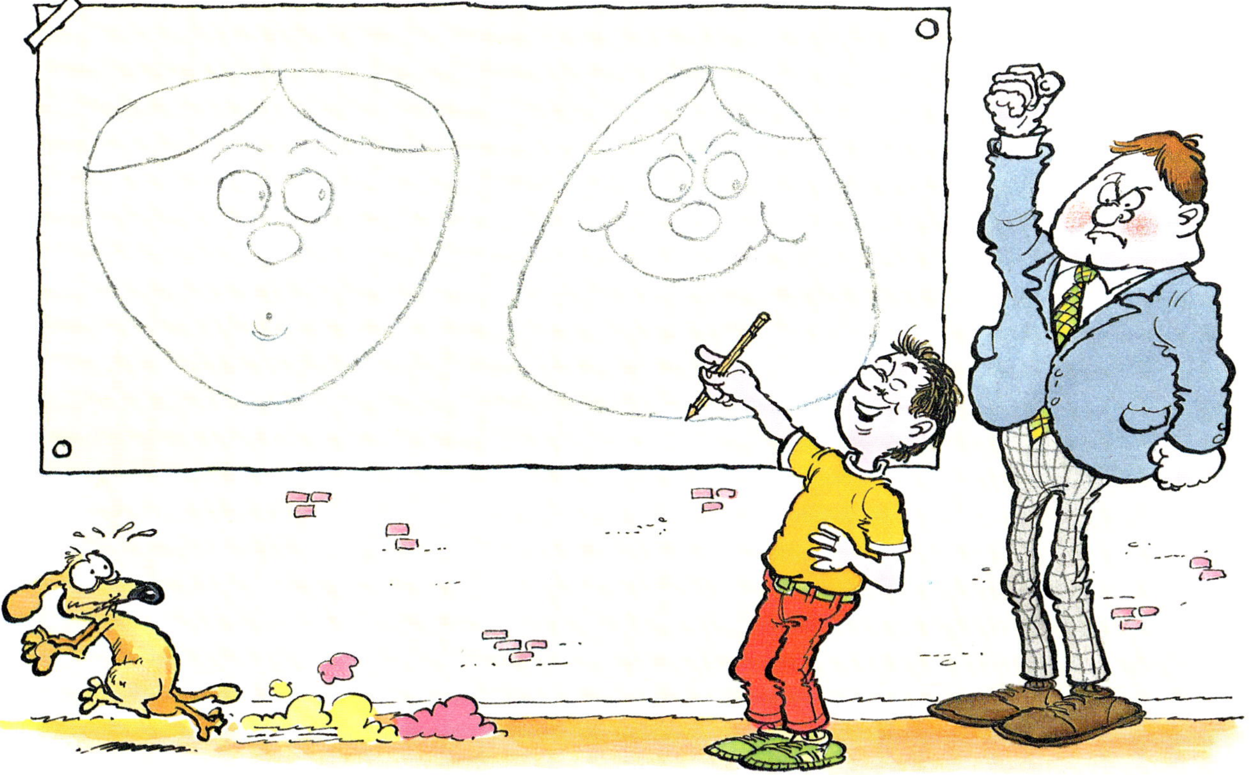

A PERFECT MATCH

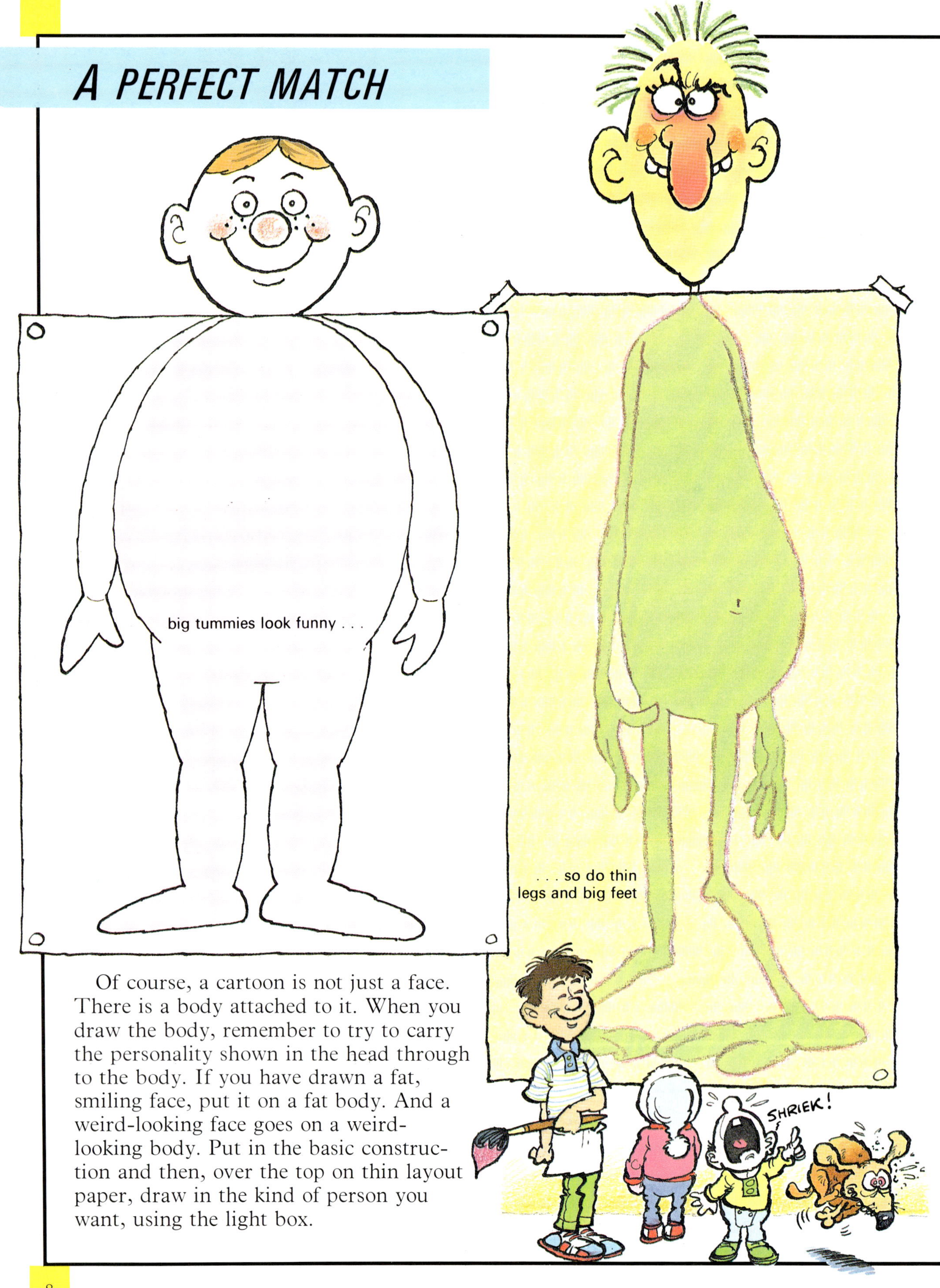

Of course, a cartoon is not just a face. There is a body attached to it. When you draw the body, remember to try to carry the personality shown in the head through to the body. If you have drawn a fat, smiling face, put it on a fat body. And a weird-looking face goes on a weird-looking body. Put in the basic construction and then, over the top on thin layout paper, draw in the kind of person you want, using the light box.

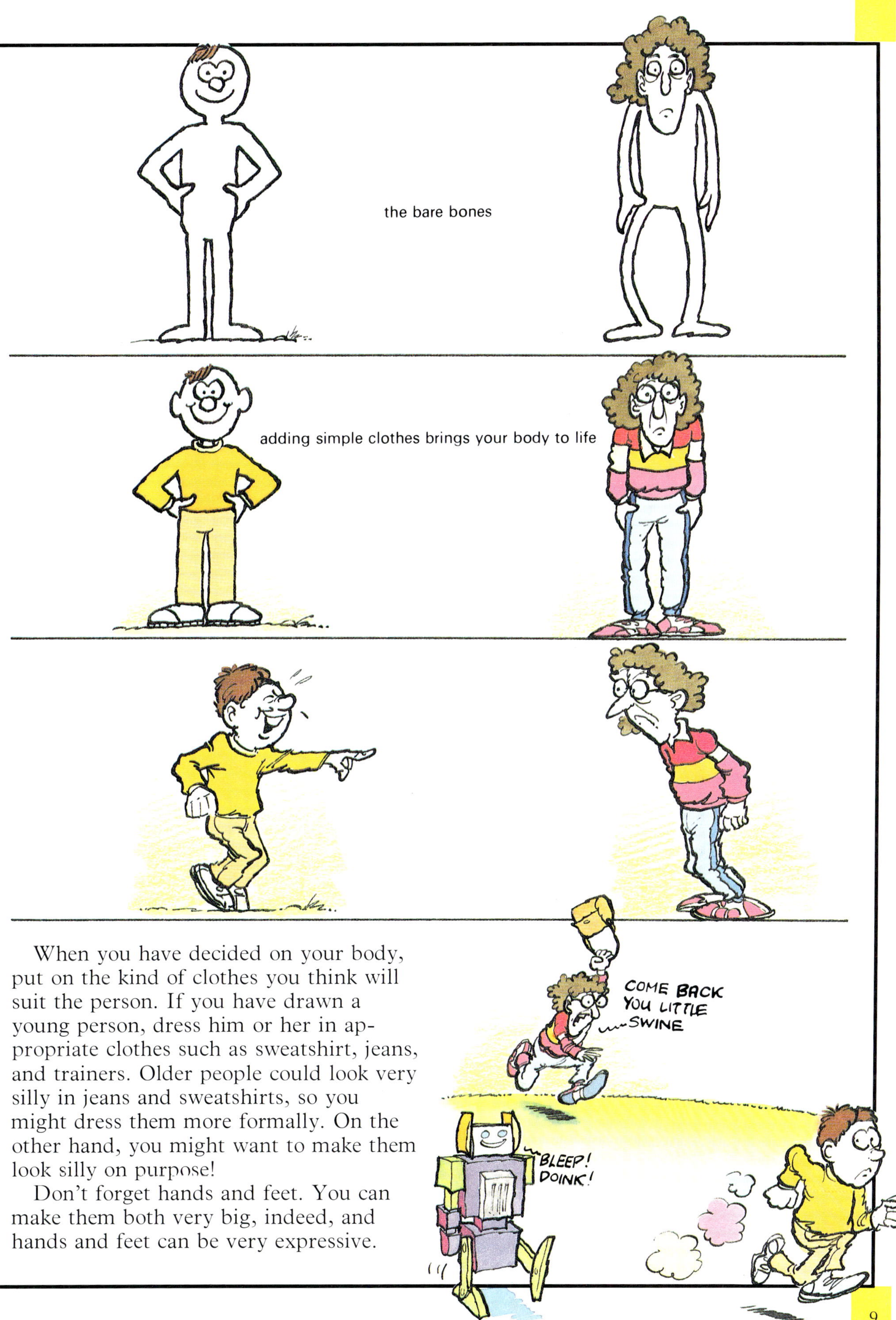

When you have decided on your body, put on the kind of clothes you think will suit the person. If you have drawn a young person, dress him or her in appropriate clothes such as sweatshirt, jeans, and trainers. Older people could look very silly in jeans and sweatshirts, so you might dress them more formally. On the other hand, you might want to make them look silly on purpose!

Don't forget hands and feet. You can make them both very big, indeed, and hands and feet can be very expressive.

ZOOMING ALONG!

So far, you have drawn your figures so that you are looking at their fronts. And they have been stationary.

Now you have to make the drawing turn. This will mean that an arm or a leg will be partly hidden behind the body.

When you do the basic construction, always draw in the whole arm or leg. Then, when you come to trace over the construction, just leave out the bits that you won't see.

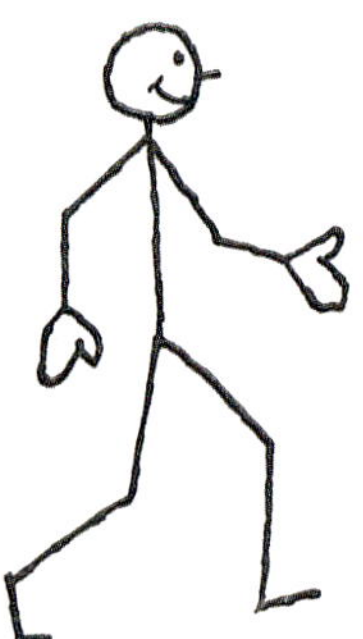

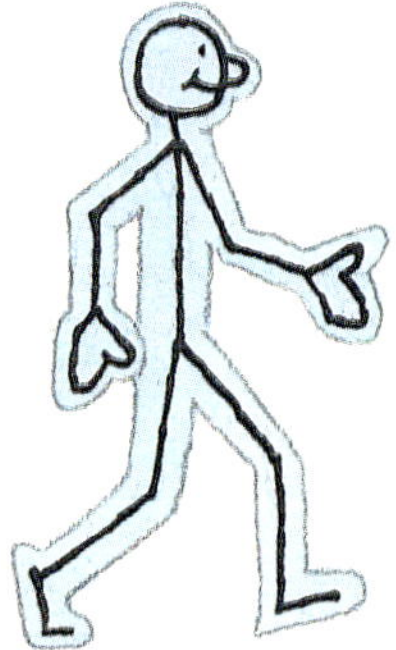

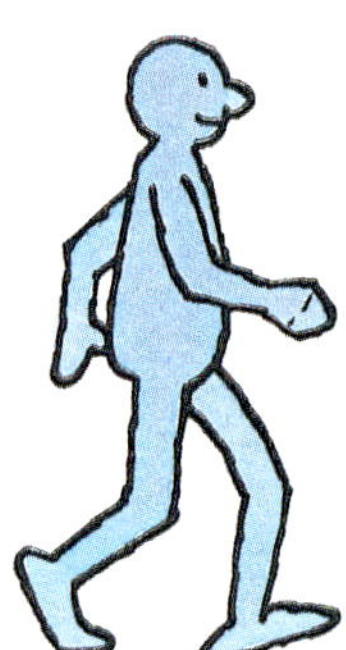

It is quite easy to make a figure move. Start by drawing a stick figure walking along. Think about the way you walk. Notice that your left leg moves forward together with your right arm. So draw the stick figure in that position. Using this figure as your 'model', draw a cartoon figure in a similar pose. Now try to make the stick figure run and, using it as your model again, draw the cartoon.

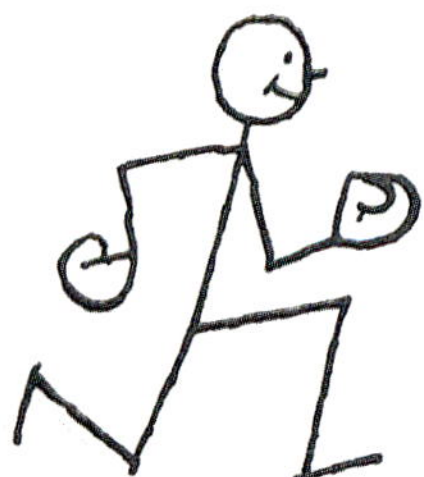

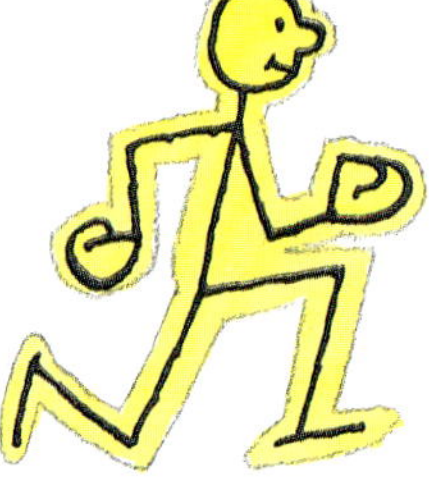

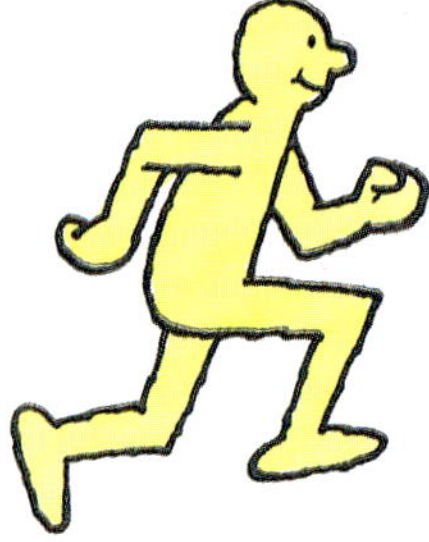

In general, to make their point, cartoonists draw very extreme action. For example, if the figure is running, it should be really zooming along. So you should emphasize the action.

Here is what you would normally do if you were running along.

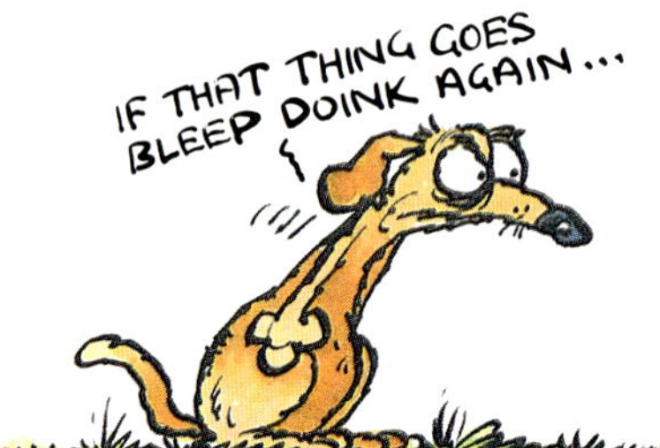

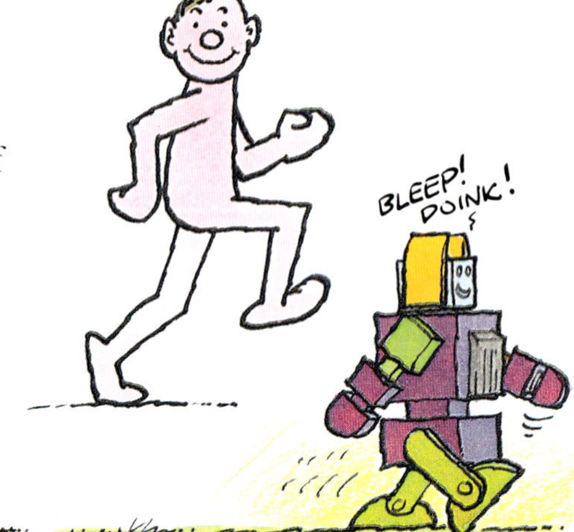

But here's what a cartoonist would draw if he or she was told to draw the same action.

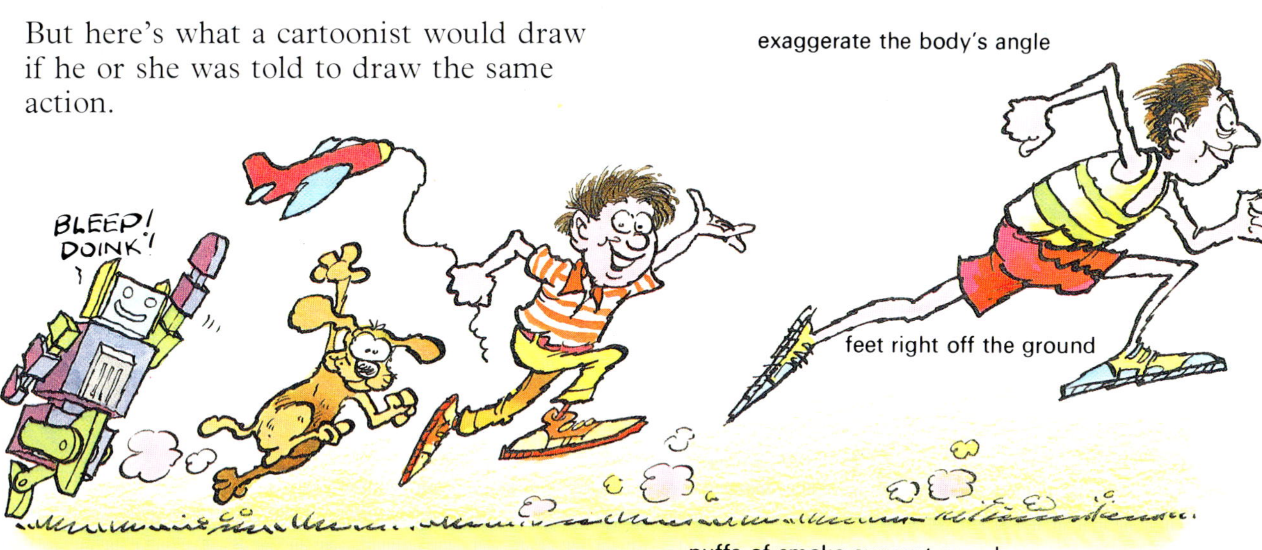

Experiment with your stick people. Make them do all kinds of different types of actions, and then construct your cartoons around them.

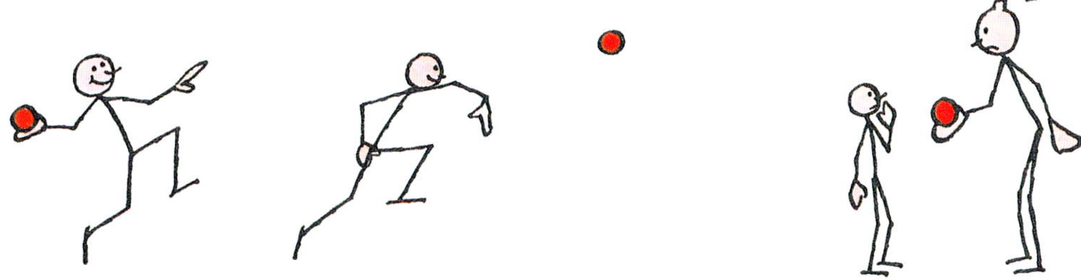

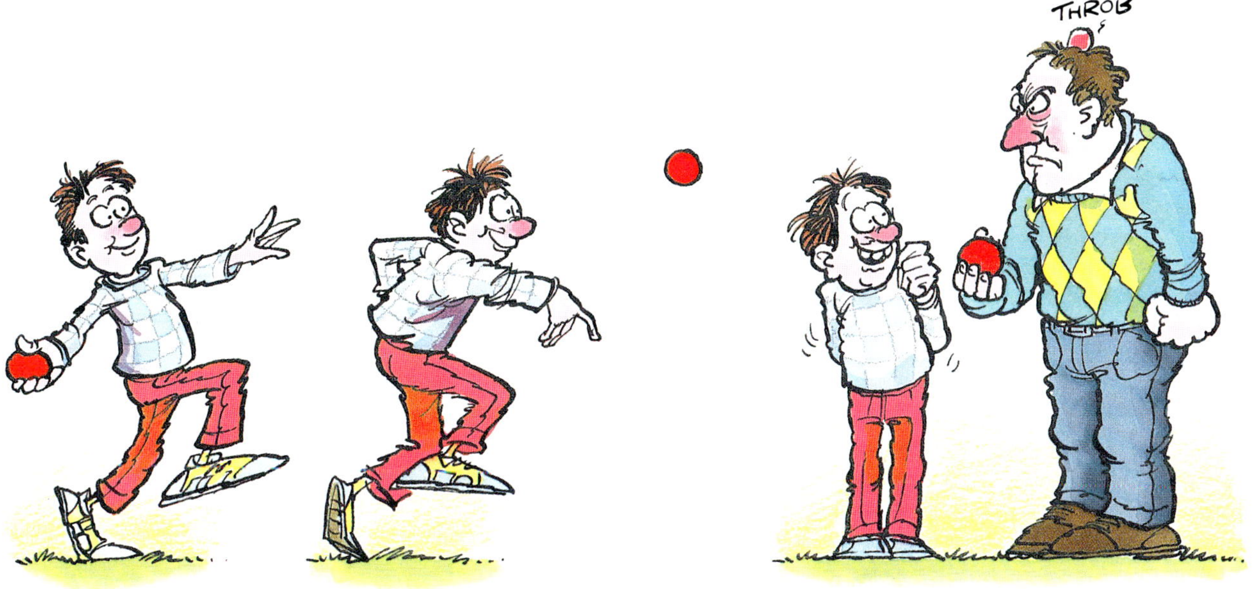

HOW TO DRAW ANIMALS

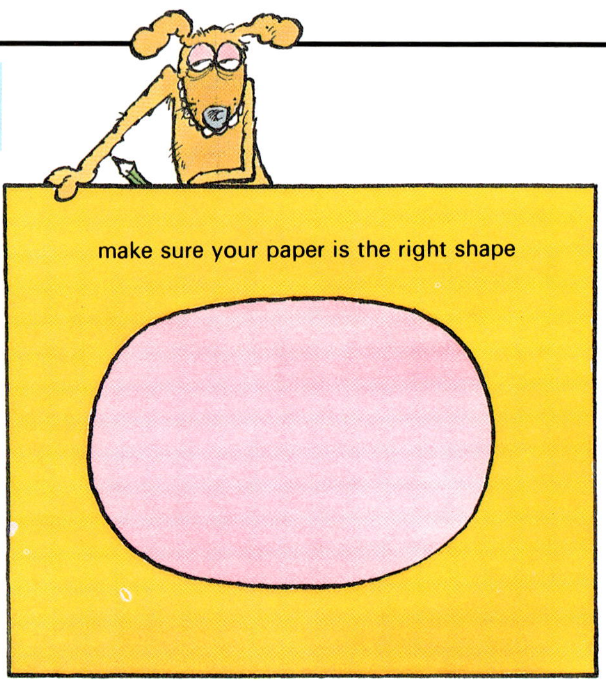

The method for drawing animals is exactly the same as the one used for drawing the human figure. Taking into account the obvious differences in the various animals that we all know, you can use this method to draw almost any animal.

As with the human figure, start with the body.

Then add the head, neck, and legs.

If the animal has a tail or a trunk, now is the time to put them in.

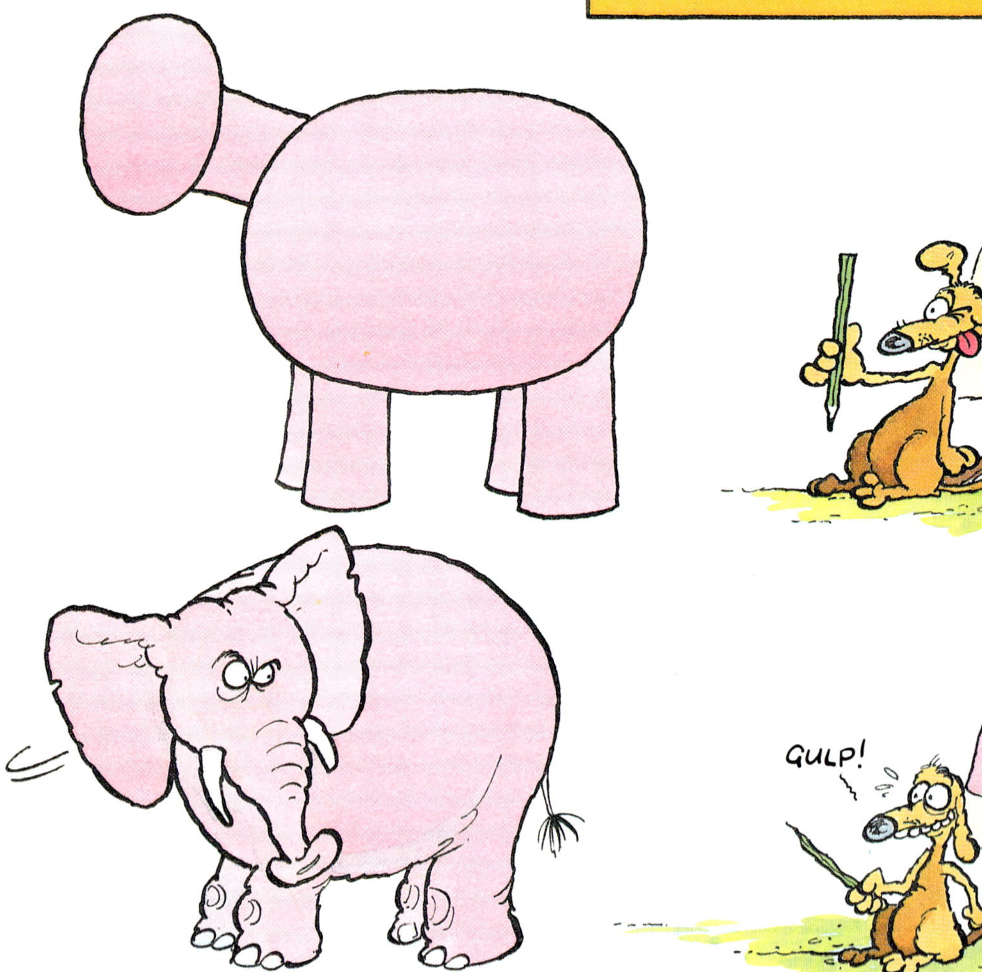

You can use the methods we have already talked about to change their expression; after all, most animals do have two eyes, a nose, and a mouth.

Do not be put off by being faced with having to draw an animal. As with the people you've already drawn, once you have the basic shape of your creature, you can then help yourself by looking in a book at a photograph of the creature you are drawing.

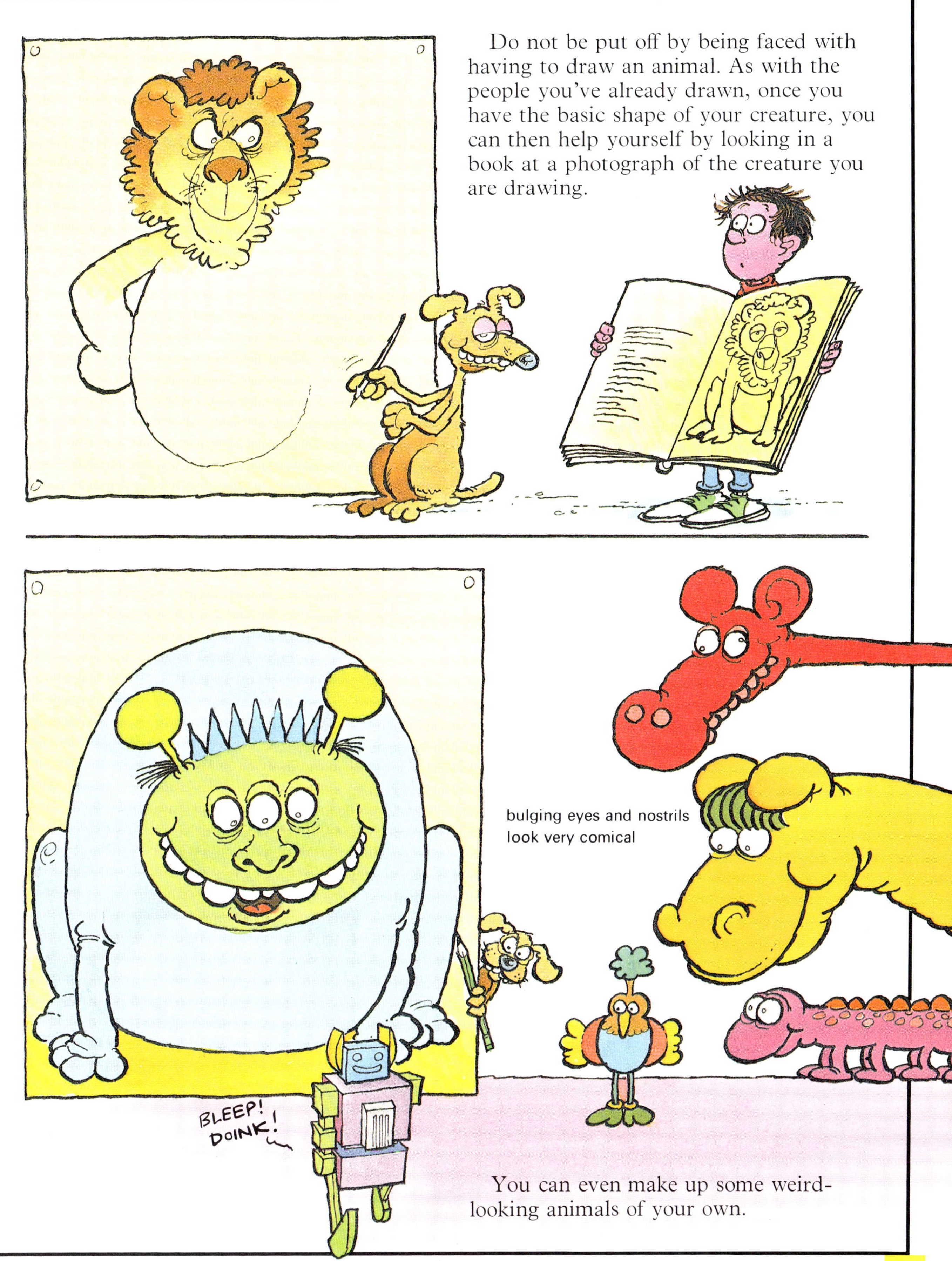

You can even make up some weird-looking animals of your own.

CRASH! BANG! WALLOP!

Although your cartoon is beginning to take shape, it still needs more action to bring it to life. There are various 'tricks of the trade' to achieve this.

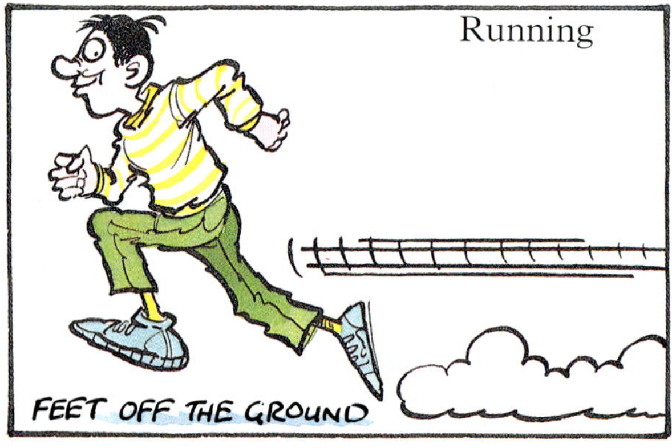

Running

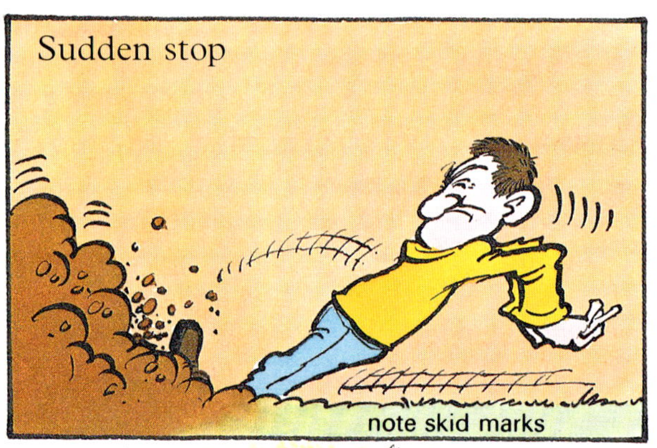

Sudden stop

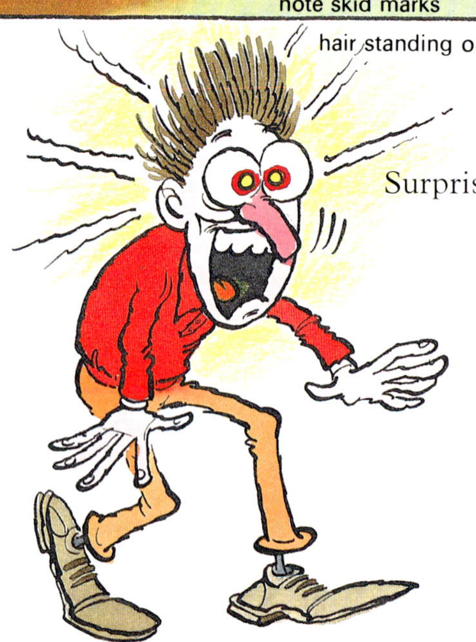

Surprise

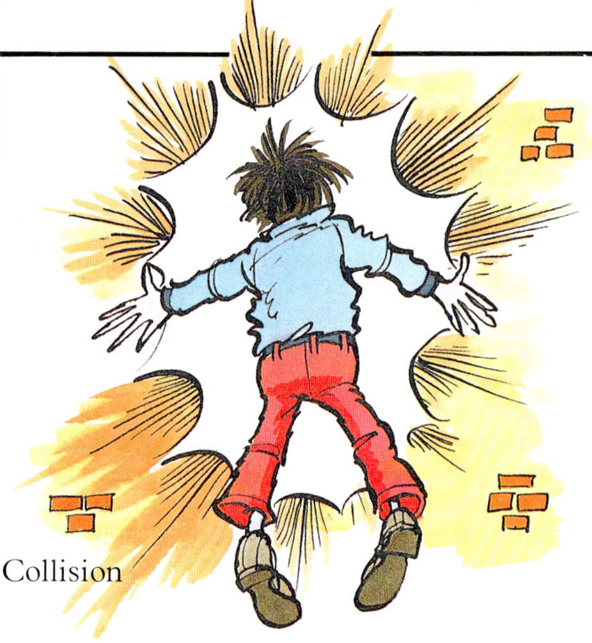

Collision

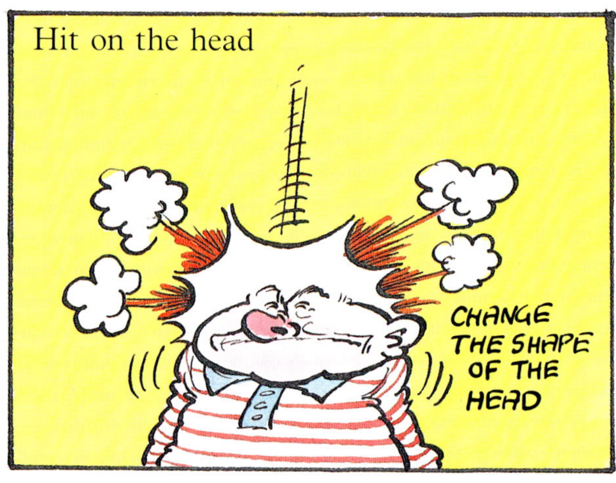

Hit on the head

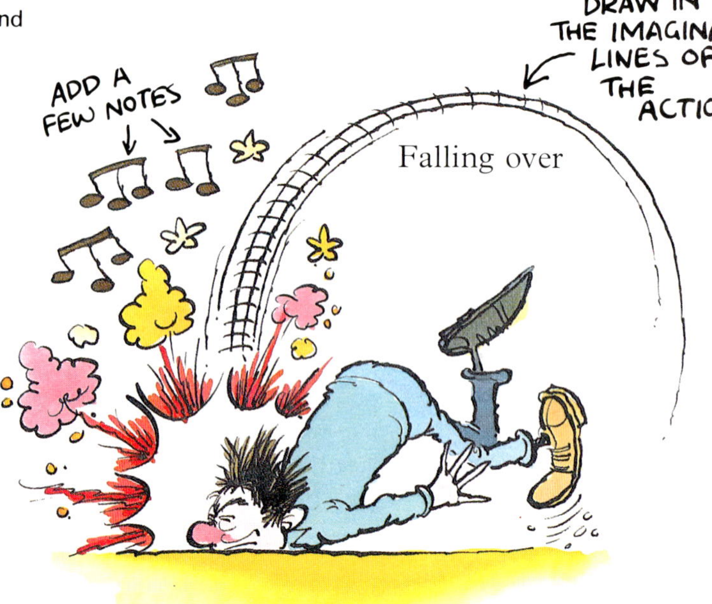

Falling over

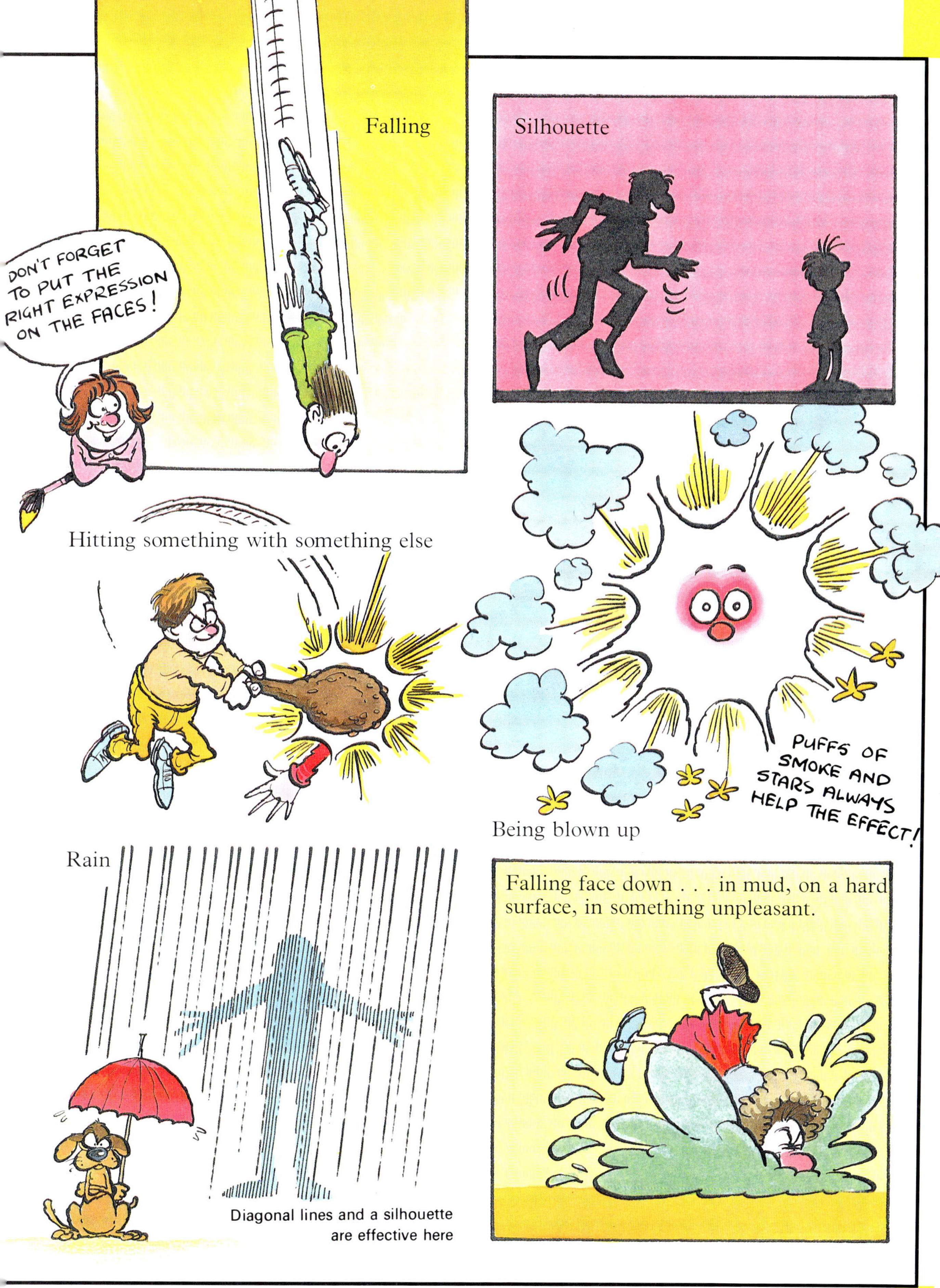
Falling
DON'T FORGET TO PUT THE RIGHT EXPRESSION ON THE FACES!
Silhouette
Hitting something with something else
PUFFS OF SMOKE AND STARS ALWAYS HELP THE EFFECT!
Being blown up
Rain
Diagonal lines and a silhouette are effective here
Falling face down . . . in mud, on a hard surface, in something unpleasant.

HAND LETTERING

Lettering by hand is an art in itself. In your library, you will find whole books on just this subject. Here are a few easy ways to include lettering in your cartoon.

CAPTION LETTERING

Look at any strip cartoon in a comic. You will notice that all the lettering in the balloons is very easy to read. Even if it looks as though it has been lettered by hand, these days, much of it is done by computer. Also 'instant' lettering is available from many shops. Many cartoonists prefer to letter their own work, however.

There are no rules about what kind of type you should use. You can make it all capitals, or you can use capitals and small letters. You can make it roman (upright) or italic (sloping).

ITALIC Roman

CAPITALS

Provided your lettering is very clear, you can decide for yourself. Always rule in guidelines in pencil first. Now, still using a pencil, write out the caption to see how it will fit in the space available. When you are happy with the look of it, finish it off in ink or in fine felt-tipped pen.

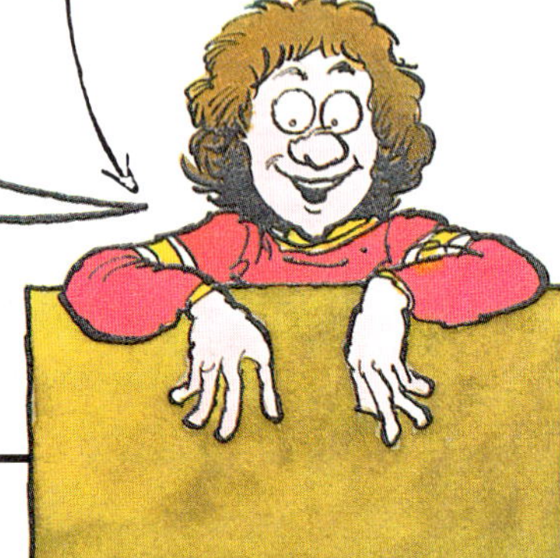

SOUND LETTERING

The other kind of lettering that is used in cartoons is what I have called 'sound lettering'. This lettering simply adds to the effect that you are trying to draw. You can draw the lettering in any way you want, provided you can read it clearly and that it conveys the word or action that you are describing.

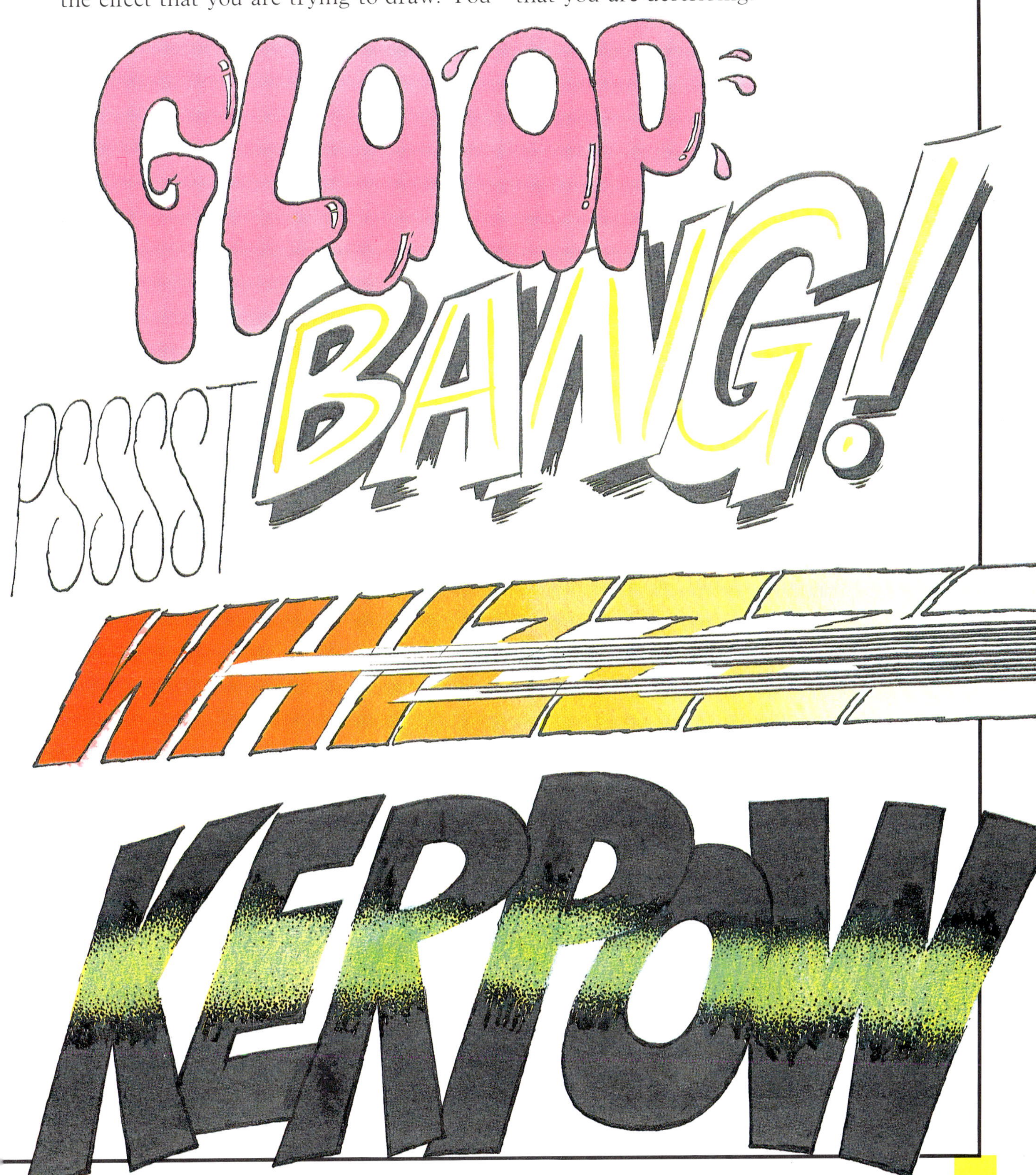

STRIP CARTOONS

At first glance, it looks very easy to draw a strip cartoon. A published comic strip takes about four professional people to put it together, however; the editor, a writer, an artist, and a lettering artist. You will have to be quite well organized if you are going to produce your own strip.

First, you must write the 'script'. Try to think of the character first and then write the story. A long story should contain about twelve to fourteen frames, a short one three or four. Leave one frame at the beginning for the title.

Now you have to draw up the 'grid'.

Here is a sample of one page that will take about twelve frames.

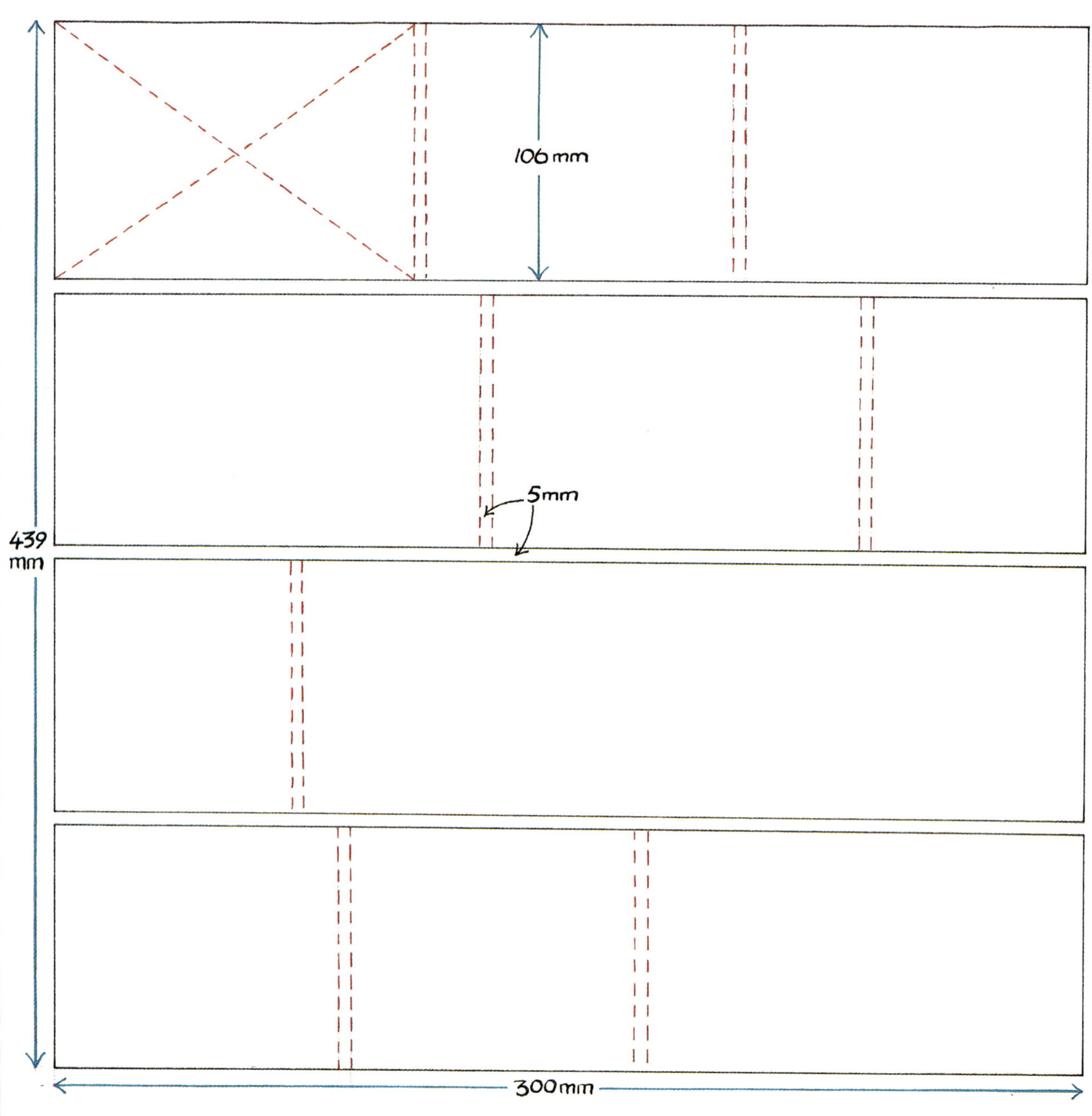

Strip cartoons are drawn much larger than they will appear in print. This is to make it easier for the cartoonist to draw it. Let's look at the script to see how many frames you have written. In this case, you find that you have written eleven frames. Look at the grid and you will see that there are four rows of pictures. That will give you three rows of three pictures and one row of two. This tells you that you should try to place the pictures in the text with the most action, on that row. So the pictures will be much bigger. The pictures with hardly any action will be very small.

When you start drawing, you must allow for the speech balloons to be drawn in. Always position the drawing in the bottom two-thirds of the frame. The action should move from left to right – the way you read. Make the action very clear and simple, so that the point of your story is easily understandable at the first glance.

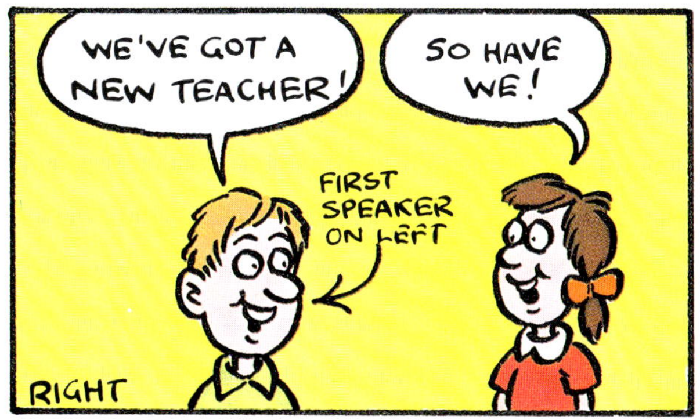

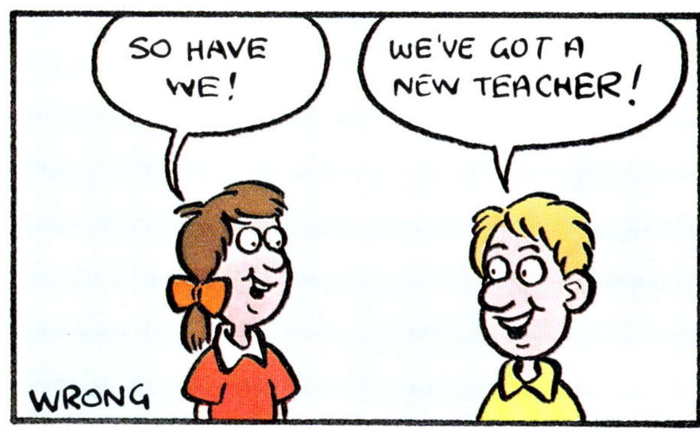

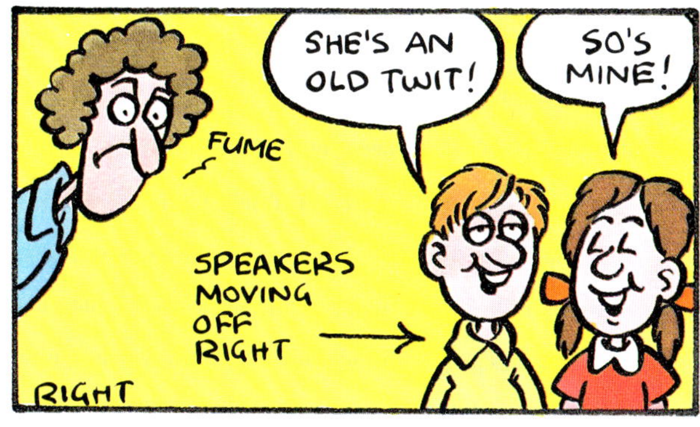

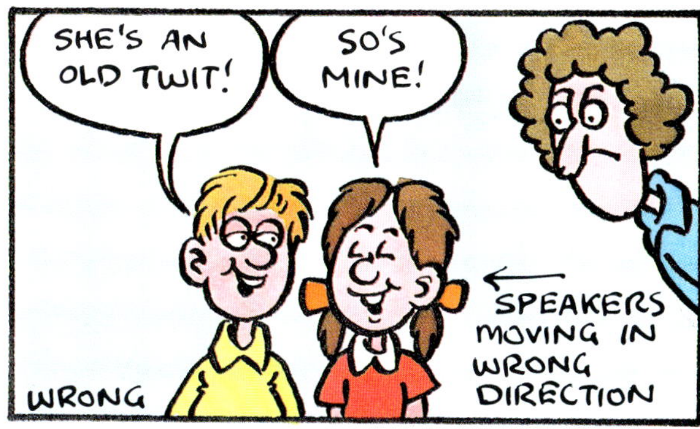

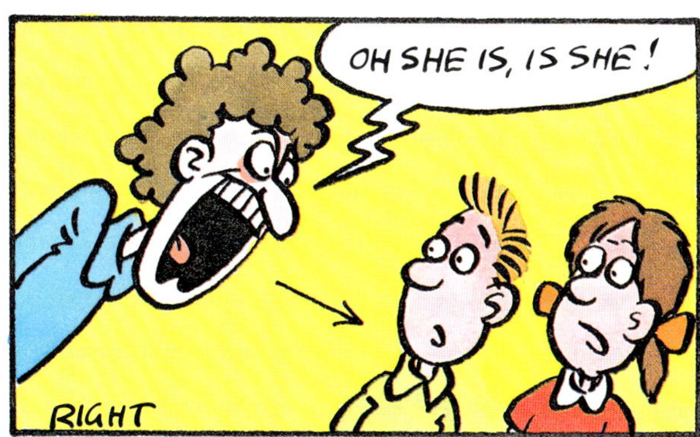

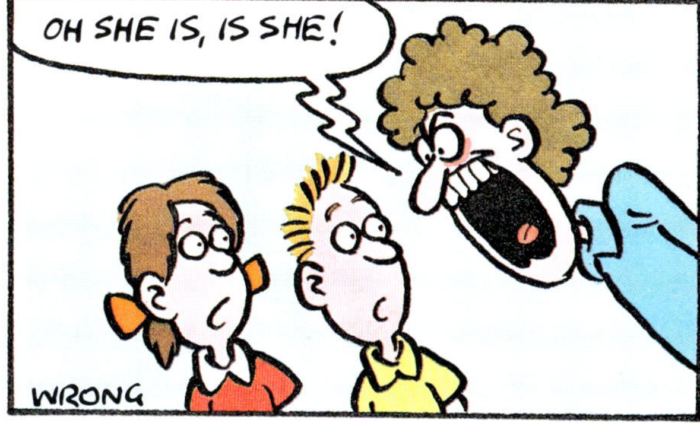

When you have finished pencilling it in, put the caption lettering into the balloons and make the speech mark from the balloon come directly from the mouth of the person who is speaking. Now you can ink it in.

ANIMATION

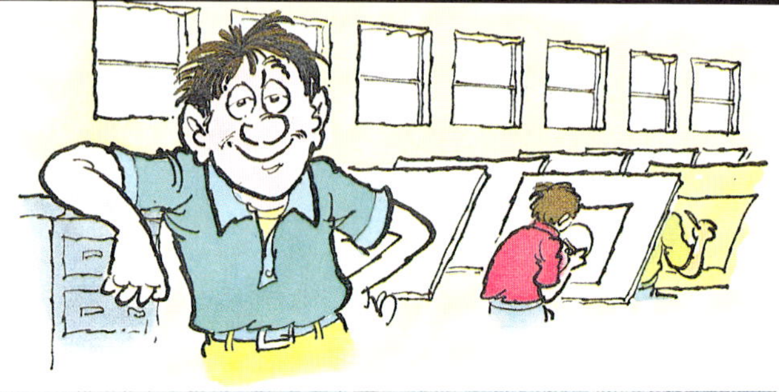

Animation is quite different from drawing 'cartoon illustrations'. Animated cartoons are very expensive and take a great many experienced people a lot of time to produce.

There is a way that you can make your own 'moving' pictures that isn't expensive at all. And, with the help of your friends, you can have lots of fun. You can certainly make a moving picture on your own, but it is quicker if there is another pair of hands to help. The process is very easy, but you must do it in the right order. You will need your light box, cartridge or quite stiff paper, and a felt-tipped pen.

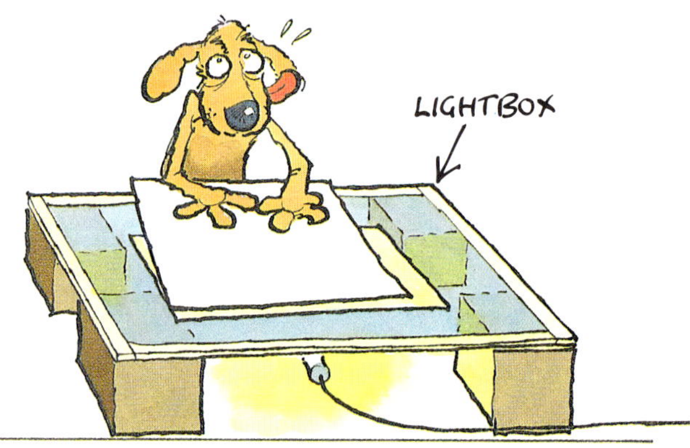

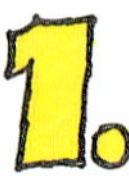

Draw a rectangle in the middle of a sheet of paper and tape it to the top of the light box. Draw a grid.

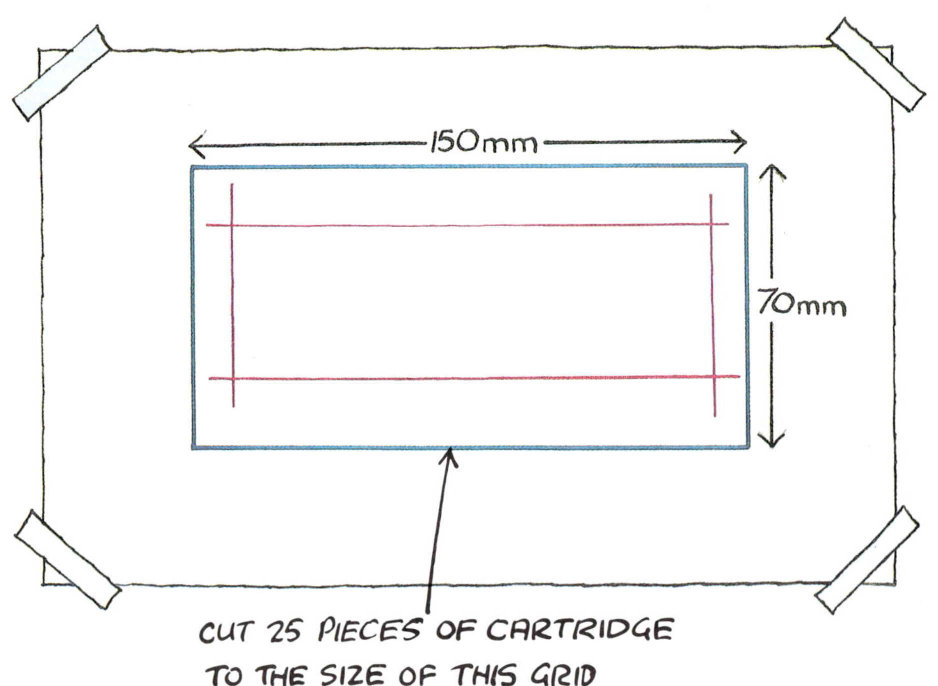

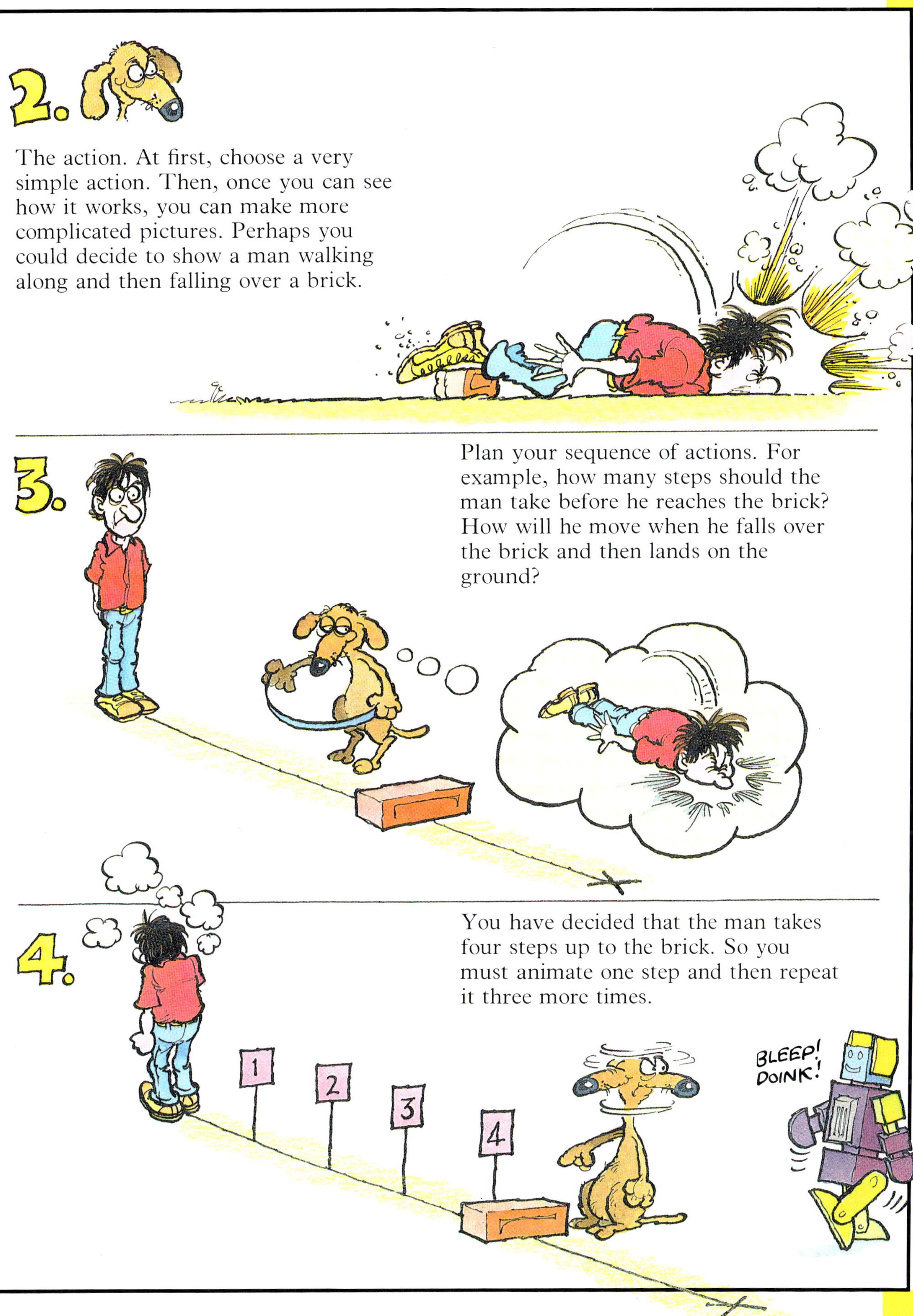

2.

The action. At first, choose a very simple action. Then, once you can see how it works, you can make more complicated pictures. Perhaps you could decide to show a man walking along and then falling over a brick.

3.

Plan your sequence of actions. For example, how many steps should the man take before he reaches the brick? How will he move when he falls over the brick and then lands on the ground?

4.

You have decided that the man takes four steps up to the brick. So you must animate one step and then repeat it three more times.

ANIMATION 2

Now, break the one step by deciding how many movements will go into each step. The general rule is that, if you put in more steps, the movement will be slow, less steps and the movement will be quick. Decide that the man is moving quickly, and put in five steps. Draw the first movement, the last movement, and then the three between. Repeat this series of drawings three times for the three steps.

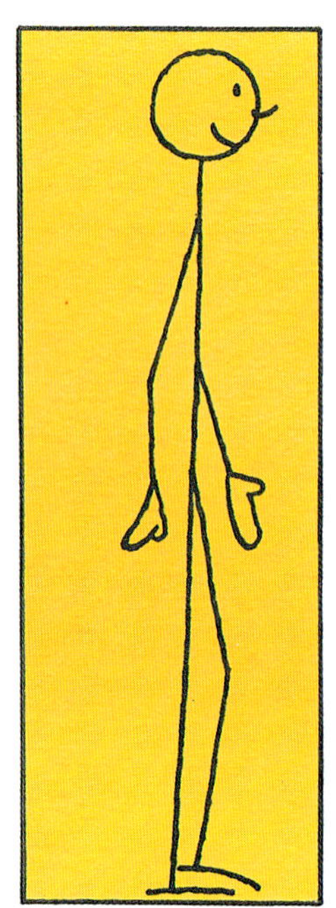

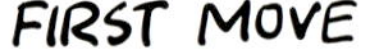

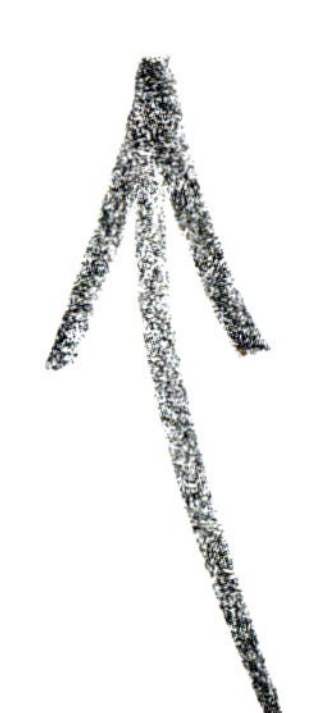

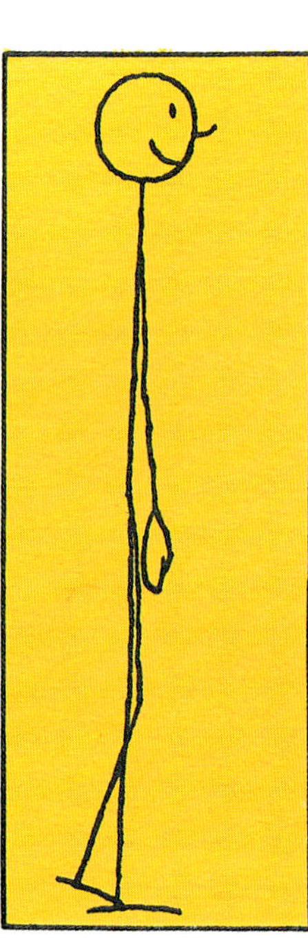

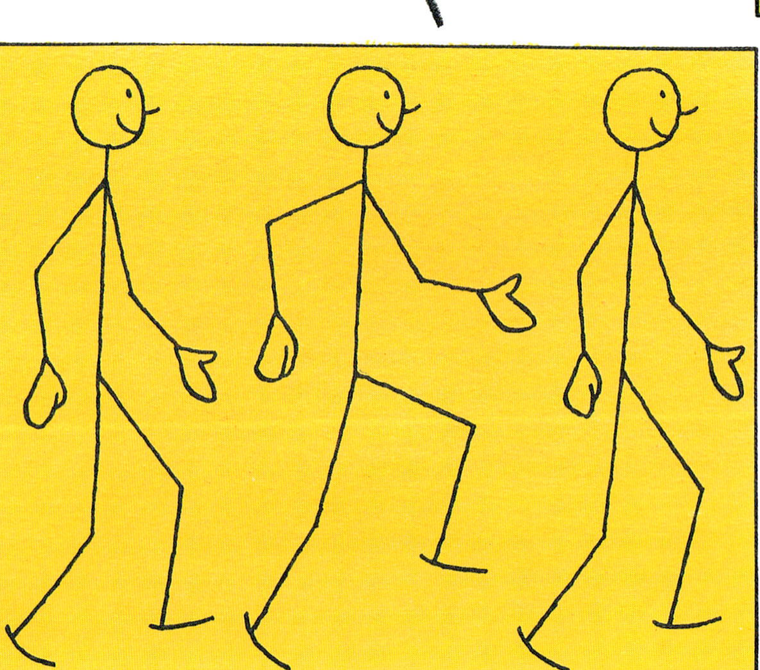

YOU CAN PUT IN MORE STEPS IF YOU THINK THE MOVEMENT WILL BE SMOOTHER.

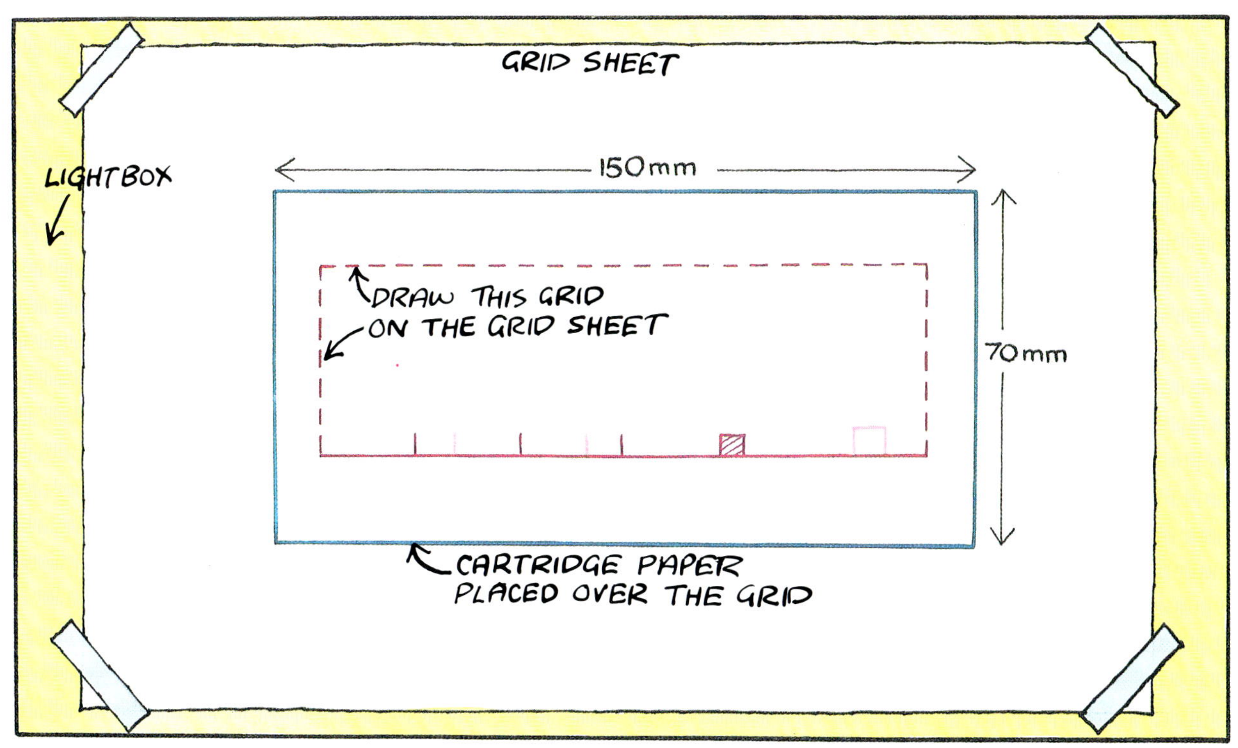

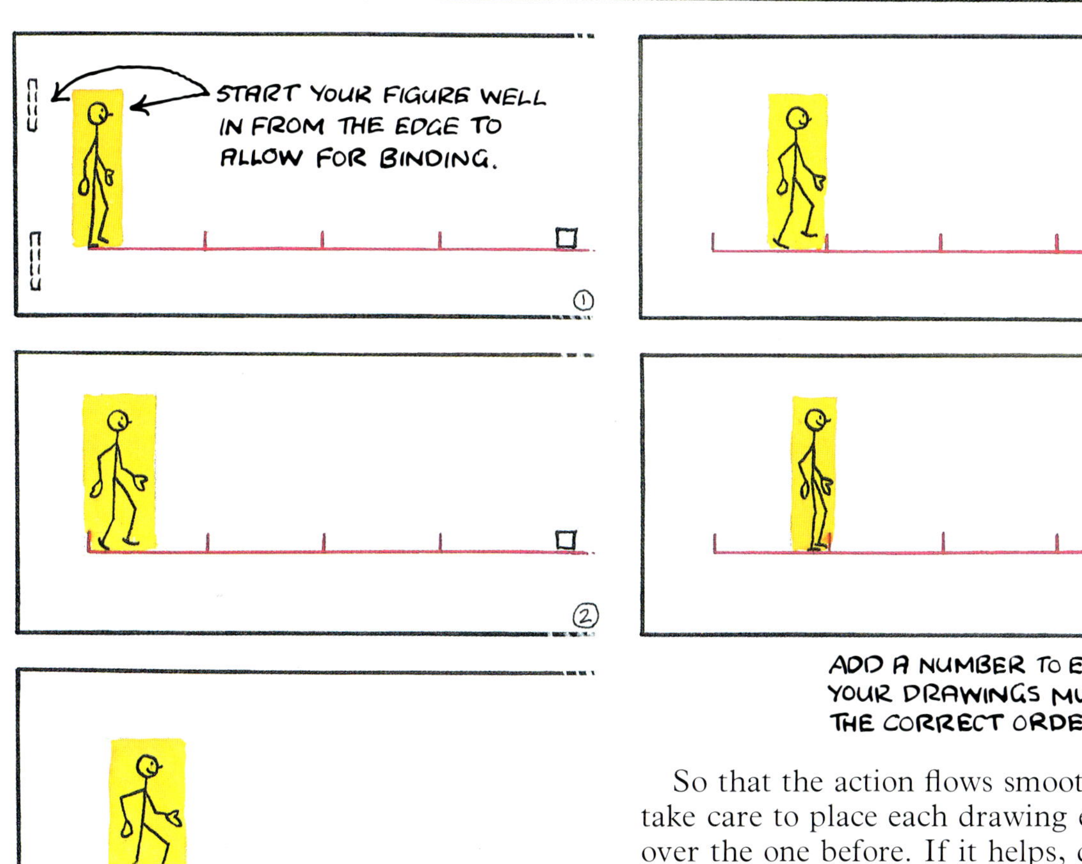

So that the action flows smoothly, take care to place each drawing exactly over the one before. If it helps, draw two parallel lines, and then place your figure between these lines.

ANIMATION 3

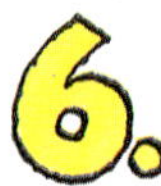

It is a little more complicated to make your man fall over the brick and land on the ground. Draw the first action, and then put in the last action. Now, divide the sequence still further, and draw what you think the figure will look like in the middle of the fall. That done, you can add one or two more stages before and after this central action. That's the job completed.

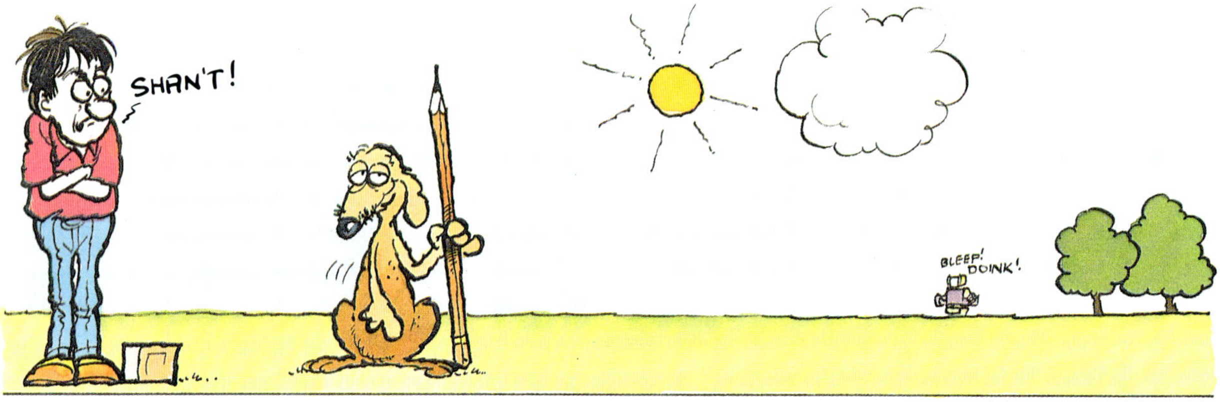

SHAN'T!

BLEEP!
DOINK!

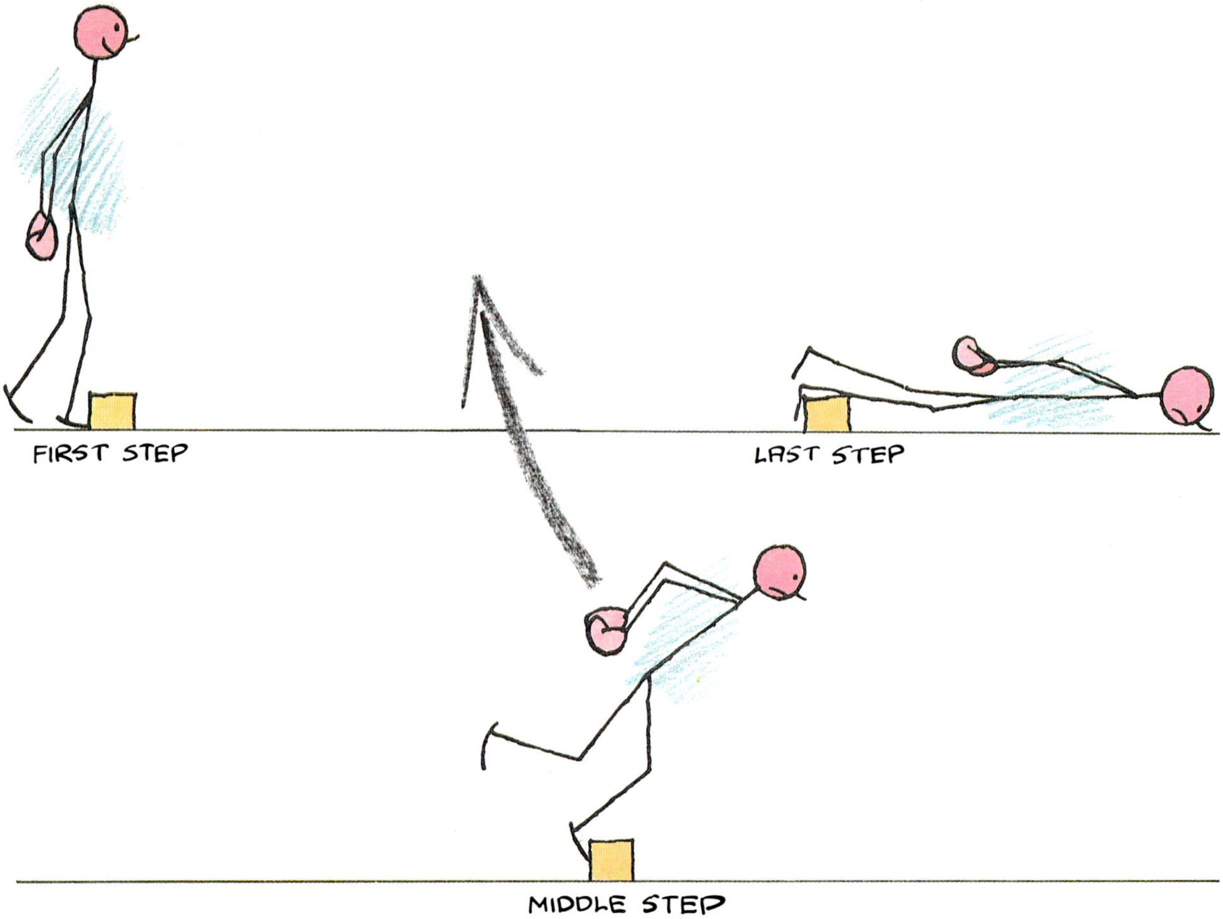

FIRST STEP

LAST STEP

MIDDLE STEP

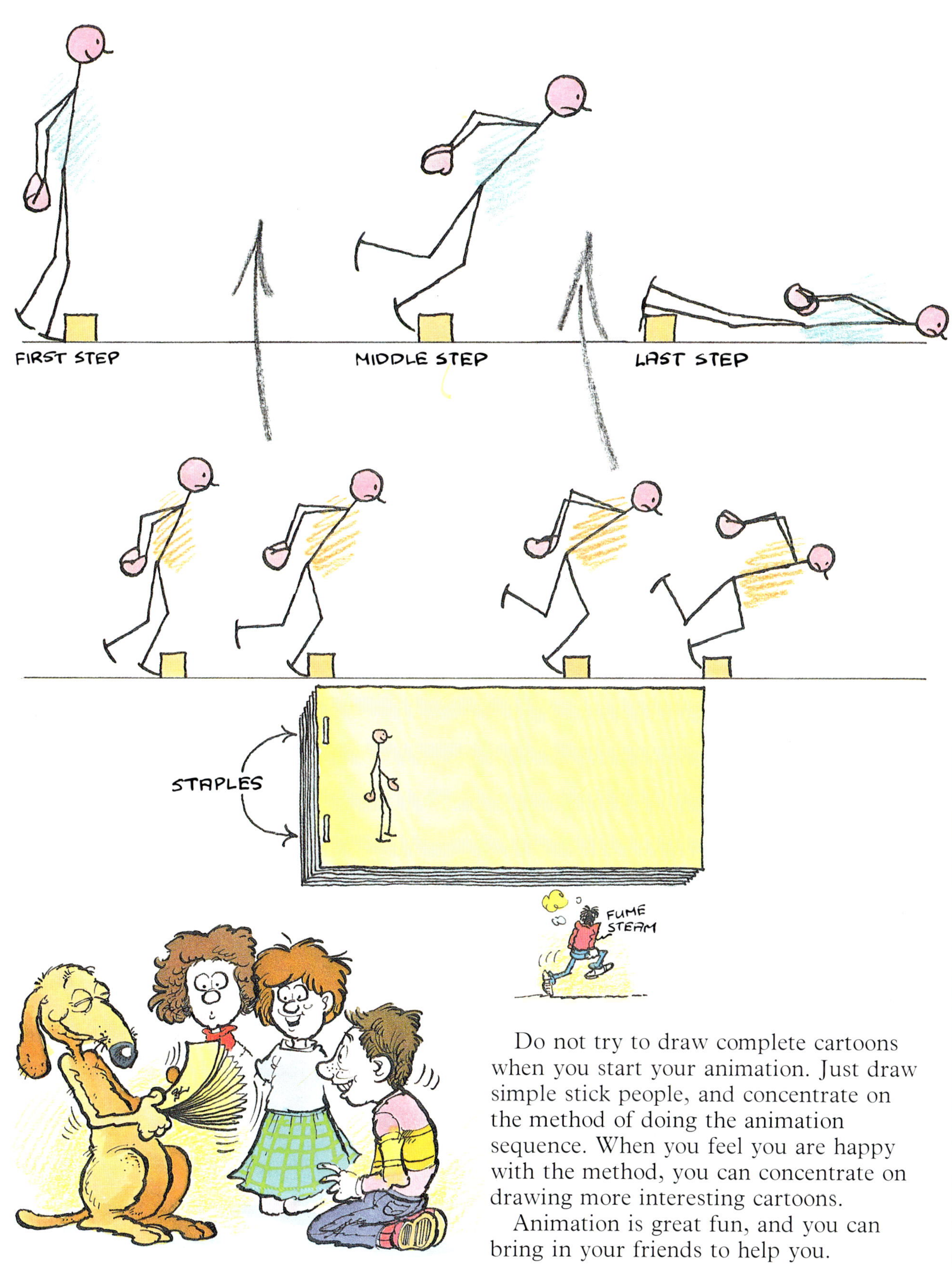

Do not try to draw complete cartoons when you start your animation. Just draw simple stick people, and concentrate on the method of doing the animation sequence. When you feel you are happy with the method, you can concentrate on drawing more interesting cartoons.

Animation is great fun, and you can bring in your friends to help you.

HASN'T AUNTY VERA GOT A BIG NOSE?

Drawing caricatures is another branch of cartooning. The secret of drawing a caricature of someone is to try to decide what is the most prominent feature of that person. Whenever you hear of someone being talked about, try to imagine him or her in your mind. For example, Uncle Fred is very fat or Aunty Vera has a big nose. It is this that makes the caricature. Concentrate on that main feature. Then draw your cartoon, and make that feature very prominent indeed. You can distort the face as much as you like. In fact, the more you do, the better it will be.

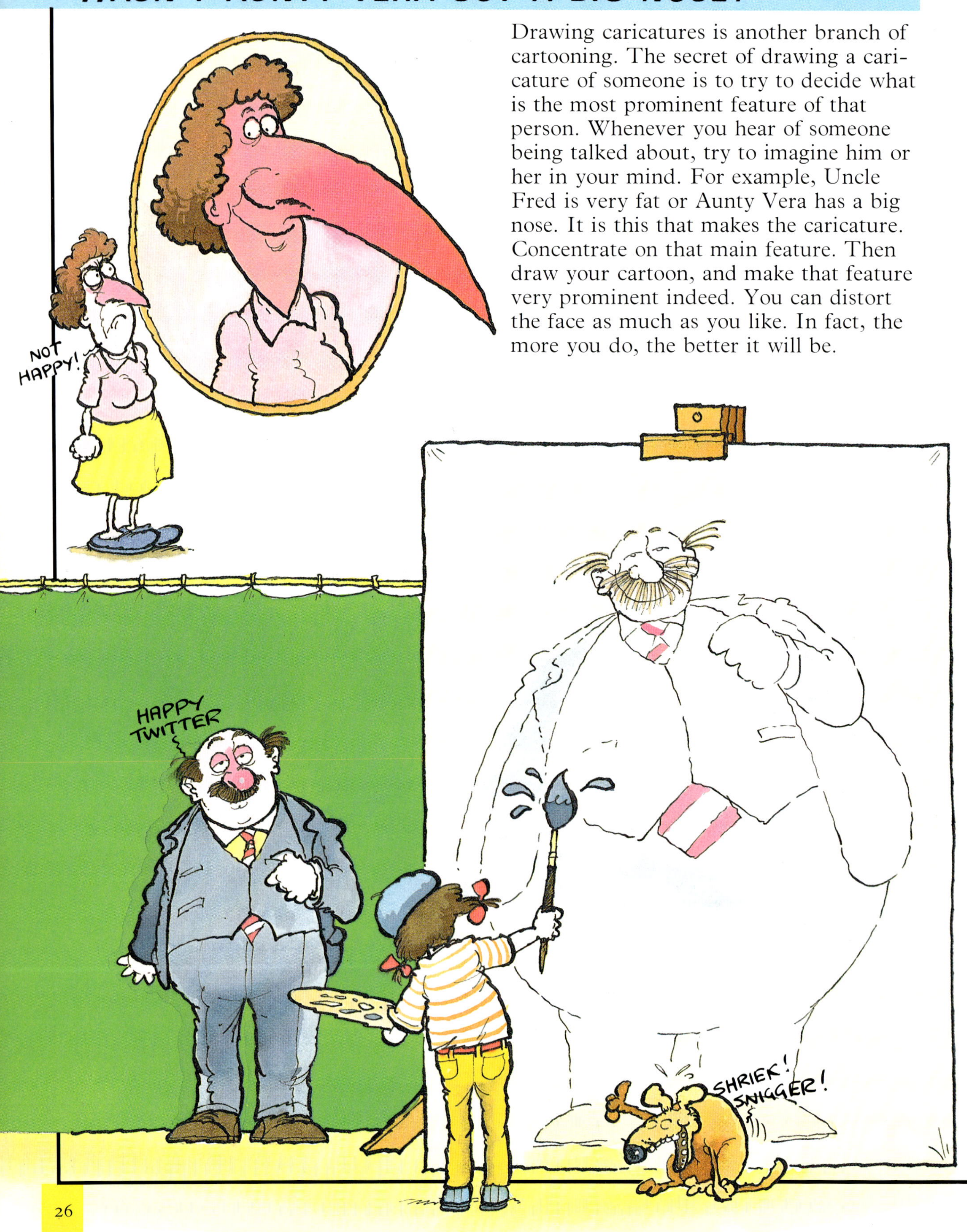

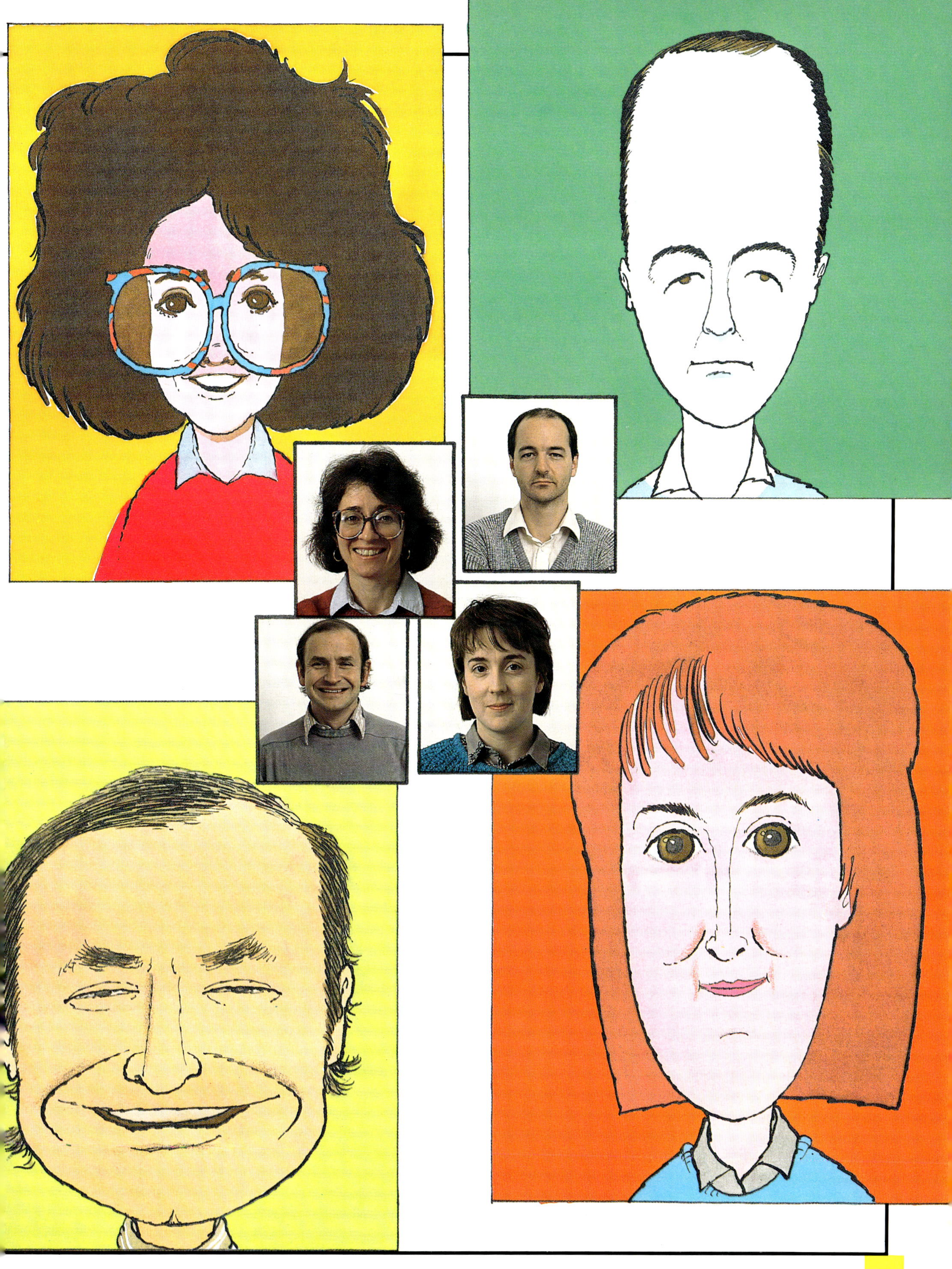

COLOURING IN YOUR CARTOON

Cartoons are usually coloured with very bright, flat colours. There are various ways you can do this.

Provided you have used waterproof black felt-tipped pen or waterproof ink, you should have no trouble. It is better to use quick-drying colours, such as coloured felt-tipped pens and coloured inks. Opaque watercolours, such as gouache, are also perfectly good but they take longer to dry, and you do have to mix all your colours.

MAGIC MARKER

If you are using felt-tipped pens, keep strictly within the area that you are colouring. If you mix felt-tipped pen colours, they tend to look very messy. Coloured inks should also be used with care. They have the advantage that you can dilute them with water so that you can produce different tones of the same colour. Cartoons coloured in this way look very bright and clean. To give your cartoons even more interest, you can add crayon colour over the top of the inks and felt-tip colours you have used.

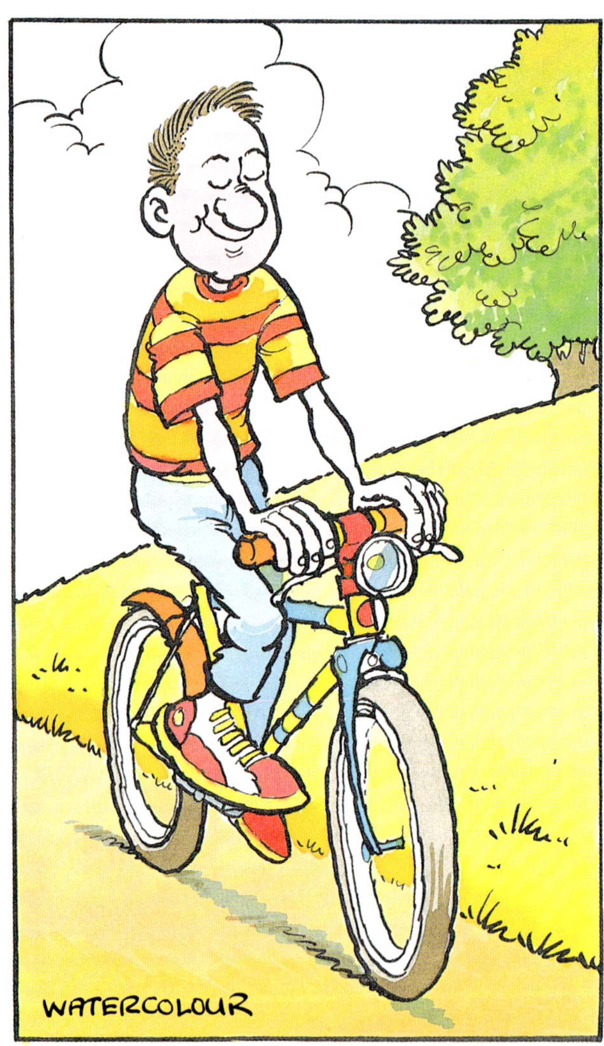

WATERCOLOUR

To add another dimension to your cartoon, try using a spray effect on the drawing. Use an old toothbrush for this.

Start colouring those areas where you know the colour, for example pink faces, green grass etc.

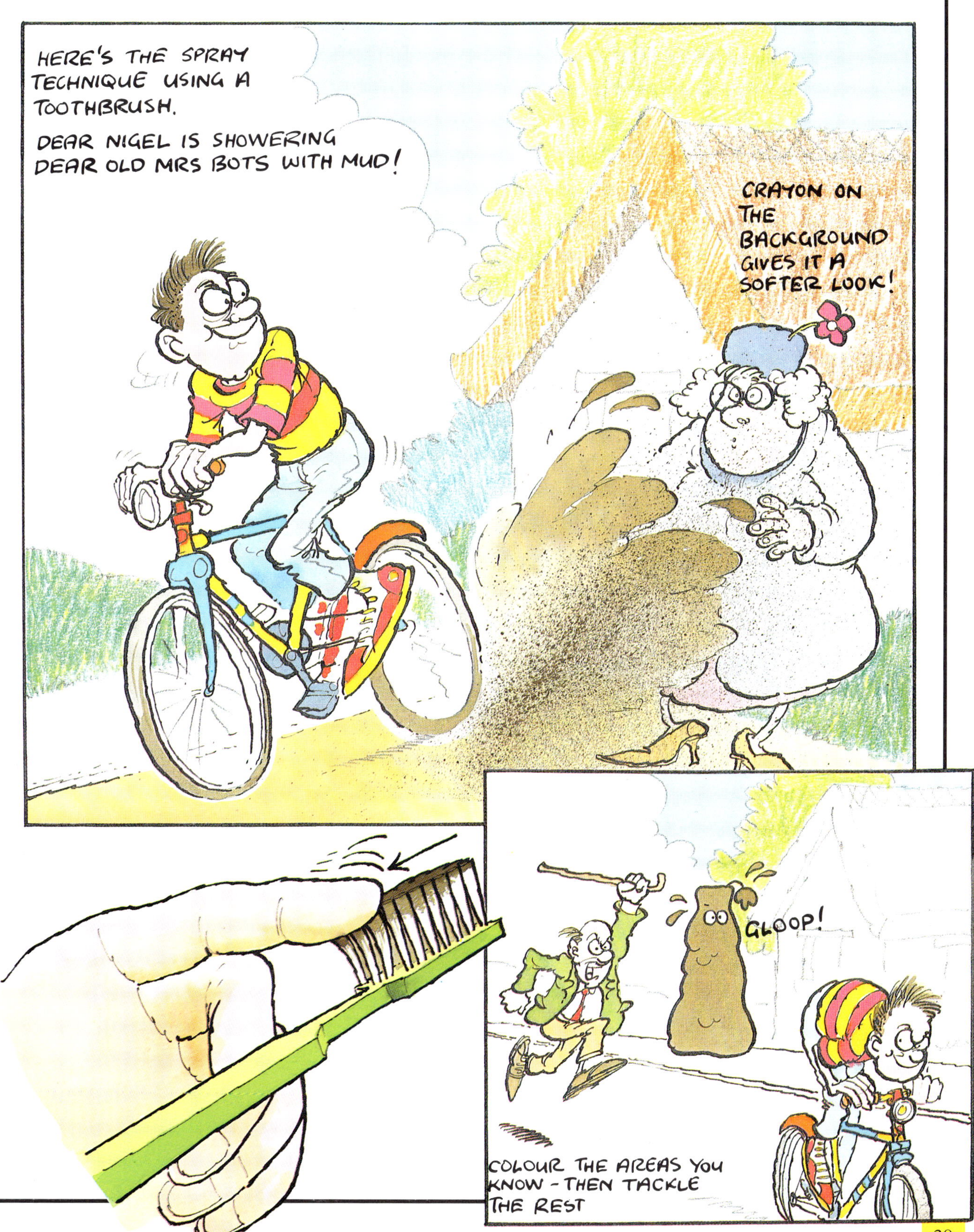

BACKGROUNDS

Backgrounds in cartoons, especially in cartoon films, are art forms in themselves. They can create a lot of atmosphere. If you look at the background to the next cartoon film that you see, you will notice that great skill and care have been put into it to create just the desired effect.

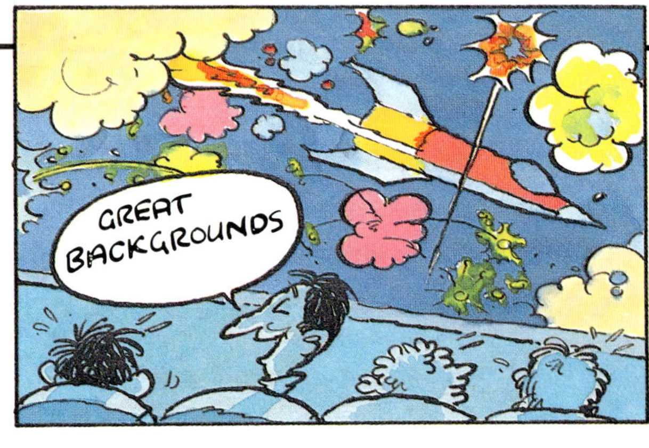

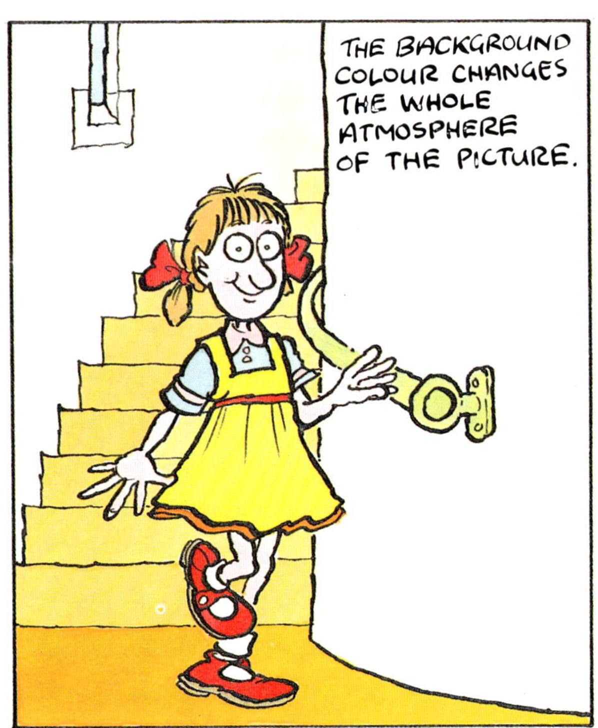

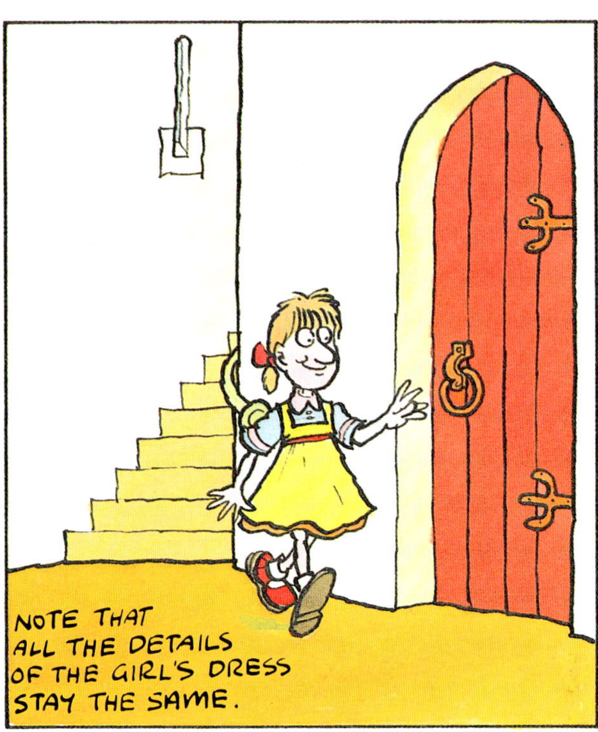

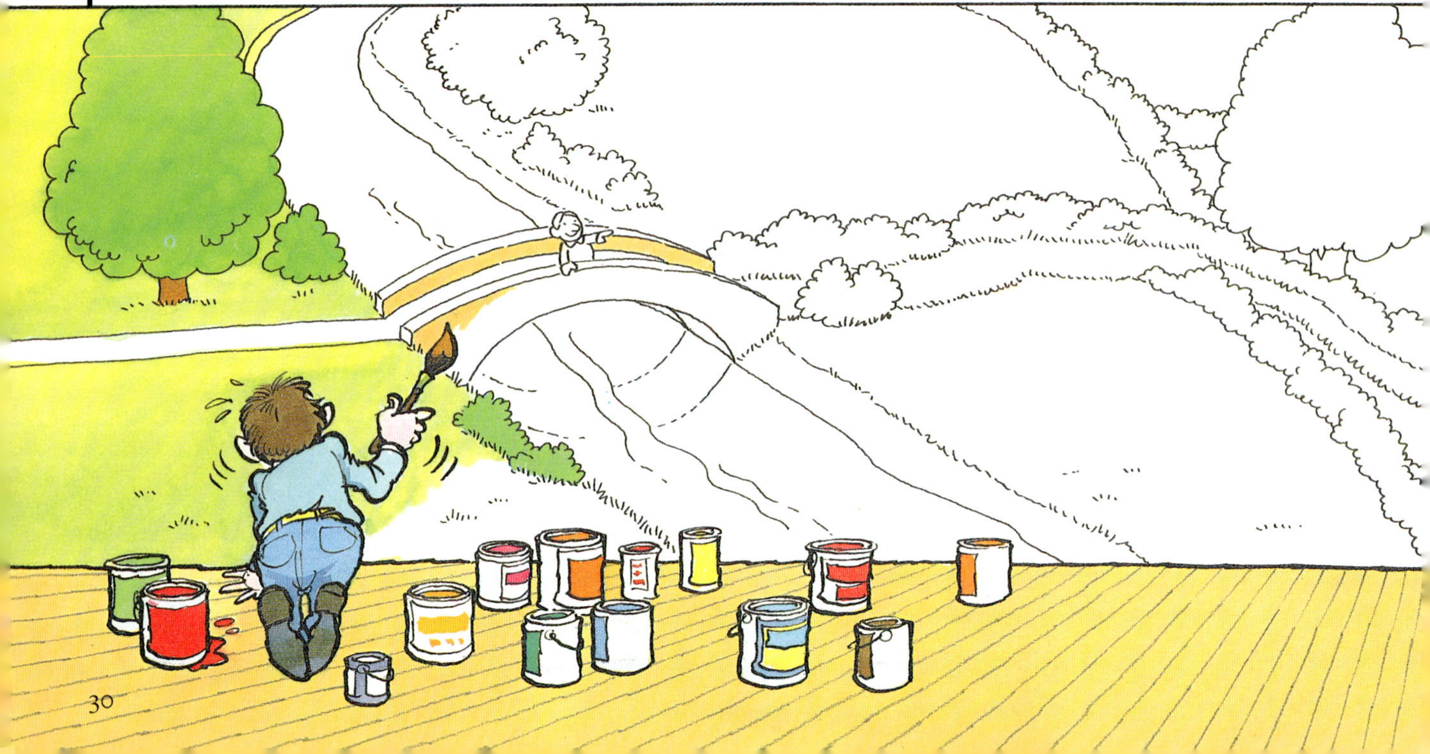

The background to a cartoon is just as important as the central figure, so do not disregard it. If you are going to do a number of drawings involving a character moving around against the same background, make certain that the detail of the background is identical from picture to picture. If you change the angle, then the background will change, but the detail will stay the same, seen from a different angle, so that the central character is always clearly visible.

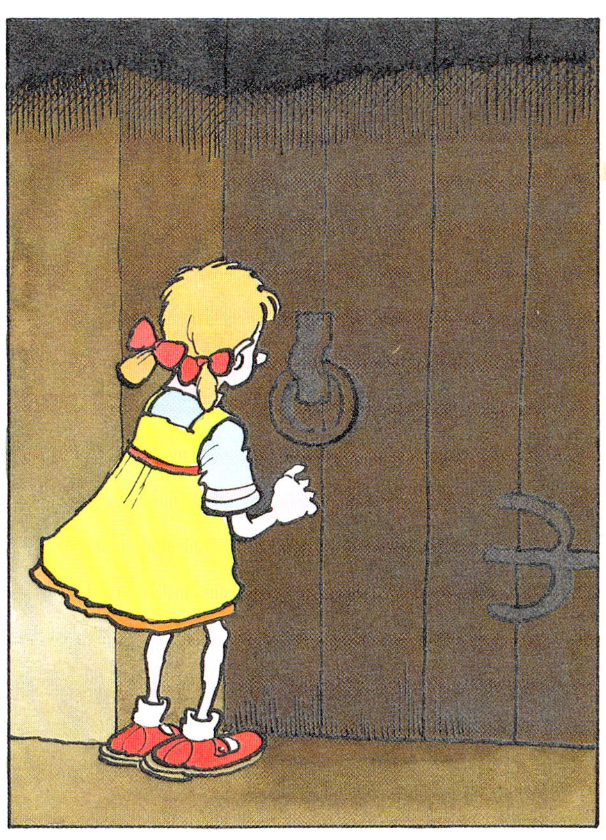

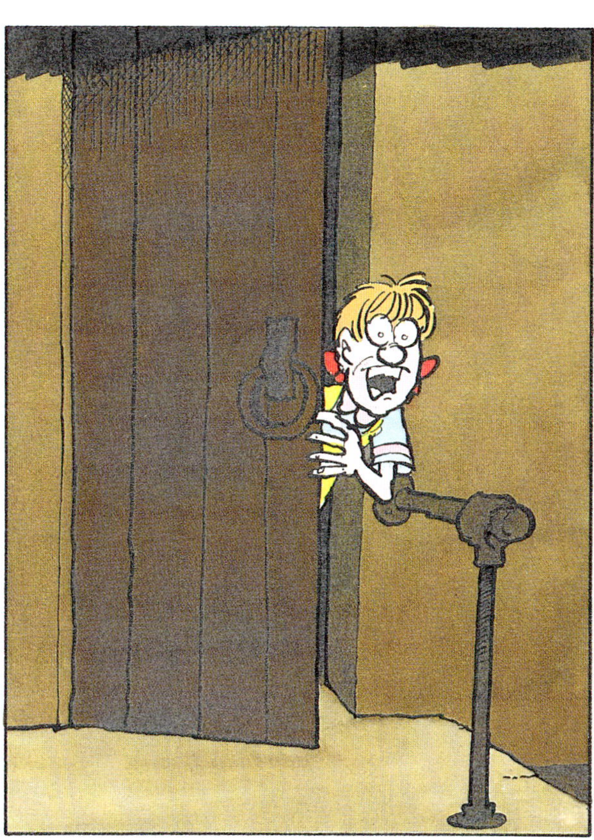

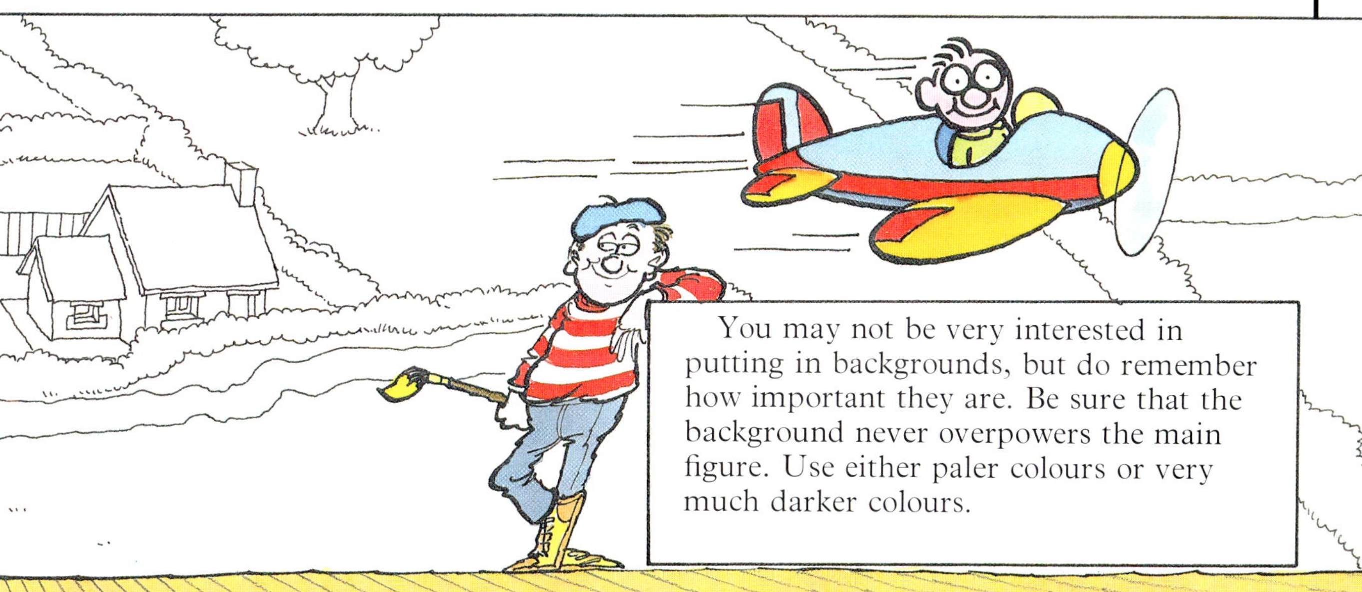

You may not be very interested in putting in backgrounds, but do remember how important they are. Be sure that the background never overpowers the main figure. Use either paler colours or very much darker colours.

Index

Action, 10–11, 14–15, 20–5
Adhesive tape, 3
Animals, 12–13

Backgrounds, 30–1
Blotting paper, 3
Bodies, 4–5, 8–11, 26
Brushes, 2

Caricatures, 26–7
Clothes, 9
Colour, 2, 28–9
Comic strip, 18–19
Crayons, 2, 28

Drawing board, 3

Faces, 6–7, 26–7

Ink, 3, 28

Kneaded rubber, 2

Lettering
  caption, 16, 19
  hand, 16
  instant, 16
  sound, 17
Light box, 3, 5, 8, 20, 23

Movement, 10–11, 14–15, 20–5

Paper
  cartridge, 2, 20, 23
  lay-out, 2, 4, 8
Pencils, 2
Pens
  dip, 2
  felt tipped, 2, 28
Putty, 2

Ruler, 3

Scissors, 3
Strip cartoons, 18–19
Studio, 3

Tissues, 3
Tracing, 5

Published in 1988 by
The Hamlyn Publishing Group Limited
a division of Paul Hamlyn Publishing
Michelin House, 81 Fulham Road, London SW3 6RB

ISBN 0 600 55538 0

Printed and bound in Italy
Front jacket illustration: David Mostyn
Illustrations: David Mostyn
Photographic acknowledgments: David Mostyn
Design: David Mostyn